2015:

THE THREATS

AND

THE WAY OUT

BY

DASHIT LUKA BUBA

2015: THE THREATS AND THE WAY OUT

Copyright c Dashit Luka Buba 2014

ISBN:10-1502368161

ISBN:13-978-1502368164

2015: THE THREATS AND THE WAY OUT

BY

DASHIT LUKA BUBA

TWITTER: @TANKHAT1

Email: progressivesarise@yahoo.com

08073741631, 08103396891

Edited by: Dr Lazarus Luka Maigoro

History & International Studies Education Unit,

Department of Arts Education

University of Jos, Nigeria

Email: maigoro2010@yahoo.com

lazarusmaigoro@gmail.com

maigorol.unijos.edu.ng

Proofread by: Eric Ganan Pam B.A,M.A,PGDE

Department of General Studies,

Plateau State Politechnic, Barkin Ladi

ericpam2002@yahoo.com

FOREWORD

In one of my papers on "Political Culture in Nigeria," I indicated that persistent general failure in the Nigerian polity can be traced to the inadequacies in the evolution of a virile political culture in Nigeria. I even suggested that specific failure of political parties, the electoral process and even governments at any or all of the three tiers or levels can be rationalized in similar terms.

However in **"2015-The Threats and The Way Out,"** Dashit has been able to convincingly identify that ethnicity, insecurity, religious bigotry, corruption, economic deprivation, insecurity, foreign influence and scramble for 2015 "Political cake" are some of the major threats to the corporate existence of Nigeria. Although, we may be tempted to say we have heard all of these before but a thorough perusal of Dashit's analysis of each of these corrosive indices working against national integration and cohesion, would convince one to conclude that the author has something new to add to what we already know or assume to know about the issues at stake.

Unlike most prophets of doom, Dashit believes that even if the corporate existence of Nigeria is under great threat, the situation can still be salvaged by four "magical wands" namely:

(i)   The return of Nigeria back to true federalism where power and resources are not concentrated in the center and where the federating units are more or less semi-autonomous powers in their own rights.

(ii.) The evolution of visionary and incorruptible leadership like we had during the era of our founding fathers who had the zeal, the will, the ability, the focus and the patriotism to move Nigeria forward.

(iii.) The possession of uncommon patriotism and zeal which will make Nigerians incurable optimists who will want to see an invisible entity where peace and progress can be easily attained by all.

(iv.) The preparedness of the Election Management Body to handle all electoral matters with due circumspection and according to the rules of the game as the conduct of elections since independence has been used to explain the major basis of political and social upheavals.

Dashit's work is not only timely but refreshingly interesting. As a historian in the making, he has presented his work at the right time when all Nigerians need to work extra hard to ensure the continuity and survival of the polity regardless of our diversities.

It is on the basis of the foregoing that I recommend this admirable and probably challenging work to all Nigerians who must be interested in the survival of the nation where all members of the heterogeneous federating units would live in peace and harmony together as one indivisible entity.

Jimoh Akanni Agboola Ph.D
Osogbo, January 2014

CONTENTS

Part One

1. Ethnicity..2

2. Religious Bigotry..................................19

3. Corruption..30

4. Economic Deprivation.........................43

5. Insecurity 57

6. Foreign Interference 78

7. Build-up to 2015 84

Part Two

8. True Federalism..................................111

9. Visionary and Incorruptible Leadership..............169

10. Credible (free and fair polls...................176

11. The Nigerian Spirit (Orientation and re-

orientation)...189

DEDICATION

This book is dedicated to the Lord God Almighty, the giver of all wisdom and inspiration, the Lord Jesus Christ my personal savior, and to the Holy Spirit, my present help, in times of need.

I also dedicate it to all those who dare to dream and to work assiduously for the Nigerian project; we shall get there.

Also to all fallen heroes who sacrificed their lives in the course of working to better the welfare of others. I dedicate this work to the memory of Late Micheal Kasham Hirse, a believer in the education of the younger generation. As a beneficiary of his benevolence, I eternally remain grateful. I also dedicate this to late Alhaji Bremah Yakubu Toknung Biandi, the Wazirin Pankshin whose memories are still very fresh in our hearts because was was such a great personality. His legacies shall be passed on to the forthcoming generations. He was such a mentor of worth.

This book is also dedicated to the memory of the late Pa J.Y. Lot, who, tirelessly and consistently, would wake us all up early in the morning[wake up and wash], and to be fed with spiritual food[quiet time],mostly against our adolescent will, but now we know better. How I wish he was here. Rest on in the Lord's bosom till we meet to part no more.

ACKNOWLEDGEMENT

Special appreciation to my parents, Mr. and Mrs. Buba Dashit, my siblings Mrs. Dinatu D. Amana, Mrs. Rahila C. Datok, Mrs. Rebecca D. Bako, Mrs. Suzanna H. Aboi, Mr. Mark B. Dashit, Mr. Victor B. Dashit, Mr. Mwanlong B. Dashit and Binta Buba Dashit.

I remain grateful to Dr. J.A. Agboola who took time out of his tight schedule to o through my work and to write a foreword and also contributed his insights from years of experience making the work a masterpiece. My thanks also go to Dr. Lazarus Maigoro who edited my work, for the herculean task and putting an academic finesse to the work.

I appreciate my mentor, Bishop David Oyedepo, for impactful messages of encouragement and his books that shaped my mentality. I also thank Pastor Poju Oyemade, my dynamic and visionary mentor, Pastor Sam Adeyemi who organized Excellence in Leadership Conference where I caught this vision. I also appreciate Pastor E.A Adeboye, the mentor of mentors.

The exemplary leadership of Professor Attahiru Jega who has brought a lot of meaning into the Electoral system is equally appreciated; To Mr. Ayodele Okunfolami, Mr. Shwarji Enock Gontul and Mr. Francis Ngban a.k.a. Okadigbo, for their insightful contributions to this work. I want to specially appreciate Mr. Setle Daze who stands as a rallying point of the Daze family, and being a mentor of repute, kudos Sir. I appreciate Mr. Percy Daze, my father both in secular and in the Lord. I appreciate all my uncles, aunties, nieces, cousins, nephews, in-laws and all my friends. Thank you all. I appreciate the support of Late Chief Michael Hirse and Dr. M. D.Bako; I wouldn't have been a graduate without you.

I appreciate the Love and care of Alhaji Saleh Karimu, you have always been there for me. I cannot forget COMRADE YOMI AMOO, you took me in when I needed a place and you thought me things I needed to know, you are a true comrade.

The criticisms of Ayodele Okunfolami, Mr. Setle Daze and Dr. M.D. Bako gave me focus to carry on. The encouragement and observations raised by my team (committee), gave me wings and surely I can fly. I appreciate Mr. Plangji Daniel Cishak, who chaired the committee, Mr. Jonathan Datok, Mr. Boniface Kumchi, Mr. Anfo Mann, Miss Lilian Ajinai, Mr. Victor Buba Dashit, Mr. Palang Solomon, Mr. Alex Audu Bida, and Mr. Miapsuk Ralph Madugu.

There are so many other people out there that I cannot mention here, but I acknowledge all your support, advice and the show of love.

INTRODUCTION:

REMINIESENCING INTO HISTORY

Nigeria is an oil rich country, precisely the sixth largest exporter of crude oil in the Organization of Petroleum Exporting Countries (OPEC). The country also has abundance of mineral resources spread all over the states of the federation with vast, fertile and rich arable land for agricultural production and attractive tourism potentials. Ironically, amidst all these, majority of the population are still living in poverty and starvation.

Presently, there is so much apprehension in the land. This is probably due to the issues of persistent and unchecked corruption, ethnic and religious bigotry that are polarizing the nation, economic deprivation that denies Nigerians access to their common wealth, insecurity which is currently threatening to tear the nation apart and western interest with their Nigerian collaborators who are scrambling for the control of Nigeria's economic resources.

This book is divided into two parts: Part one analyzes the threats to the corporate existence of Nigeria as a united country, while part two prescribes a workable solution that will address the Nigerian problem once and for all.

Chapter one looks at the history of ethnicity in our national politics and the current realities of ethnicity in the polity.

Chapter two looks at the history and the effects of the practice of religious bigotry that resulted in ethno-religious crisis which is still ravaging the nation.

Chapter three focuses on the various causes and types of corruption and why the fight against it has been a perpetual failure.

Chapter four, centers on the fundamental causes of economic deprivation and the aftermath to the society.

Chapter five discusses the various forms of insecurity arising from the previous threats mentioned above.

Chapter six reveals the role of the western powers in determining how our economy is run while chapter seven analyzes the activities that culminate to the build-up to the 2015 polls.

In part two, chapter eight prescribes true federalism as the way out of the log-jam. It defines federalism and how it best suits the Nigerian diversity, gives a historical account of how it thrived in the First Republic, reasons why it was thwarted and why it is the best option for now. It also looks at the economic realities that will support the practice of true federalism and the popular opinions on the same.

Chapter nine prescribes the need for a visionary and incorruptible leadership to be in place.

Chapter ten observes the imperative on the Independent National Electoral Commission (INEC), to conduct free and fair polls that will guarantee the sustenance of Nigeria into the next democratic dispensation as one peaceful united nation.

Finally, chapter eleven advocates the need for a 'NIGERIAN SPIRIT' of patriotism to be projected on the minds of every Nigerian.

PART ONE

THE THREATS

Nigeria clocked a hundred years in January 2014, but despite all threats there are strong indications that Nigeria shall survive beyond 2014 as one united Nation. A lot of threats stare the nation in the face as it seeks to maintain its stance as the giant of Africa. The threats to the corporate existence of Nigeria as outlined in this book are, ethnicity, religious bigotry, corruption, economic deprivation, insecurity, foreign interference, and the events in the build up to the 2015 general elections.

CHAPTER ONE

ETHNICITY

The first major threat to the corporate existence of Nigeria as one viable entity by 2015 is ethnicity. Ethnicity is a virus that has been causing social crises and instability in Nigeria. It has been generally perceived as a major obstacle to the country's development. Ethnicity in itself should not be a factor of divisibility if properly harnessed but persistent political/social and developmental patronage by elected leaders along ethnic lines over the years poses great threat to Nigeria's corporate existence. The foregoing statement aptly sums up the damaging implications of ethnicity for not only political stability and national development in Nigeria, but also a spate of party politics representation and its possible effects on democratic consolidation in the polity. The pattern of party politics practiced in Nigeria today is based on ethnic sentiments to the detriment of merit and objective perception of the indices which are instrumental to political stability.

These have become a source of serious concern to all true democrats. Also, appropriation of resources has further polarized Nigerians along ethnic and regional divides. It is pertinent to look at what ethnicity means before analyzing the damage it has been causing to the polity.

The term 'ethnicity' has been defined severally by different scholars according to their individual perception or their specialty in life.

According to wikipedia.org; an ethnic group or ethnicity is a population of human beings whose members identify with one another either on the basis of a presumed common genealogy or ancestry (1) or recognition by others as distinct group (2) or by common culture, linguistic, religious or territorial traits. Processes that result in the emergence of such identifications are summarized as ethno genesis.

Members of an ethnic group, on the whole, claim cultural continuities overtime, although historians and anthropologists have documented that many of the Cultural practices on which various ethnic groups are based are of relatively recent invention. The term is used in contrast in race, which refers to a classification of physical and genetic traits perceived as common to certain groups. Ethnicity is a social phenomenon associated with (communal) competition among members of different ethnic groups. And by ethnic groups in turn are formations distinguished by the communal character of their boundaries and membership especially language, culture or both, with language constituting the most crucial variable in Africa. An ethnic group, however, is not necessarily linguistic or culturally homogeneous, in so far as it often subsumes sub-cultural linguistic, dialectic, occupational and class differences, depending on the prevailing level of socio-economic development and cultural differentiation.

It can also be perceived as a sense of people hood that has its foundation in the combined remembrance of past experiences and common aspiration. It is, therefore, evidenced as observed that ethnicity is a derivative of its articulation and activation. That is, it is the existence of the group that makes ethnicity possible. Another school of thought postulates that ethnicity is looked upon as unreal, an artificial basis of identification and collective organization, conjured up by outsiders looking for efficient instrument of political and economic control. Ethnicity or ethnic groups are generally seen as socio-cultural entity "while inheriting the state, country or economic area, consider themselves biologically, culturally, linguistically or socially distinct from each other and most often view their relation in actual or potentially antagonistic terms."

These go a long way to describe the ethnicity of Nigeria which is so varied that there is no definition of a Nigerian beyond that of someone who lives within the borders of the country. The boundaries of the formerly English colony were drawn to serve their commercial and colonial interests, largely, without regard to the territorial claims of the indigenous people. As a result, about three hundred and seventy one (371) ethnic groups have been brought together by the colonialists to form the population of Nigeria. The inability of past leaders to harness the great potentials [assets] endowed in the diverse cultures has put the country's unity under consistent siege. The count of three hundred ethnic groups cited above overwhelmingly enumerates ethnic minority groups; those that do not comprise a majority in the region in which they live. These groups usually do not have a united political voice, nor do they have access to resources or the technology needed to develop or modernize economically. They, therefore, often consider themselves discriminated against, neglected or dominated. There are only three ethnic groups which have been recognized as majority groups in their respective regions: the Hausa-Fulani in the North, the Igbo in the South East and the Yoruba in the South West. These three groups comprise only fifty seven percent (57%) of the population of Nigeria while the remaining forty-three percent (43%) comprise of other ethnic minority groups. The diversification indeed poses some sort of constraint in successfully governing such an incredible variety of people who speak over three hundred different languages, and in which the same number of separate cultures desperately try to retain their identities. This has resulted in the practice of ethno-centrism arising from unequivocal issue of carving an ethnic identity as a means of survival in fiercely competitive environments. What then are the practices that constitute ethnicity and ethno-centrism from pre-independence Nigeria till date?

Ethnic Practices in Nigeria

In pre-independence Nigeria, party politics and party formation assumed an ethnic competition, and this metamorphosed into the post-independence First Republic. The Action Group (AG) developed from the political wing of the cultural association of the Yoruba educated elite; the Egbe Omo Oduduwa; the National Council of Nigeria and Cameroun (NCNC) was closely allied with the Igbo State Union and played a significant role in the internal affairs of the party, while the NPC (Jam'iyan 'Yan Arewa) was founded by the Fulani Aristocracy. In the smaller ethnic groups especially the Middle Belt which formed the Middle Zone League in the 1950s in order to project the identity of the Middle Belt groups, a local political party was often distinguishable from the cultural association, and more significantly, the division of the country into three regions for administrative convenience by the Richard Constitution of 1946, led to the development of a strong regional feeling. The consequence of this was such that by 1953, the major political parties in Nigeria NCNC, AG and NPC, were associated with the major ethnic groups and the three regions of East, West, and the North.

The formation of such regions never captured the interest of the minorities. To further crystallize the tripartite ethnic cleavages, the party leadership was structured accordingly viz: the Sardauna of Sokoto, Sir Ahmadu Bello led the NPC of the North, Dr. Nnamdi Azikiwe held the ace for the Igbo's NCNC while Chief Obafemi Awolowo led the Action Group [AG] in the Yoruba West, each representing their ethnic regional divides while the minorities were swallowed in the interest of the dominant three. This showed up in the emergence of the Middle Zone League (MZL) founded by the late Mallam Gwamna Awana, the then District Head of Kagoro and Chuwang Rwang Pam, the then Gbong Gwom Jos. It later metamorphosed into

United Middle Belt Congress (UMBC) as a strong voice to protect the interest of the Middle Belt ethnic minorities against the dual colonialism that confronted them-from that of the Hausa–Fulani and the British colonial authorities in the North. It was, however, the absence of a well-organized, strong, visionary and purposeful cross national political party with the organizational depth and durable popular support for democratic effectiveness and legitimacy that led in part to the collapse of the First Republic. However, the constitution that ushered in the Second Republic made regulations which were intended to make political parties to be national in outlook, including their operations, but party politics and formations defying all hindrances were seen to follow ethnic dimension even in line with their operations in the First Republic. However, party politics had its worst experience during the Third Republic when the military held sway. The Social Democratic Party (SDP) and the National Republican Convention [NRC] were registered by the Babangida Administration. While the SDP was popular among the Southerners, the NRC was, however, dominant among the Hausa/Fulani in the North. Most of the Middle Belt States aligned with the SDP.

The five political parties registered during the Abacha regime: Congress for National Consensus (CNC), Democratic Party of Nigeria (DPN), Grassroots Democratic Movement (GDM), National Centre Party of Nigeria (NCPN) and United Nigeria Congress Party (UNCP) were formed ostensibly to adopt their sole benefactor, Gen. Sani Abacha (Late), as their consensus presidential candidate. The parties were referred to as "Five fingers of a leprous hand" by the late Bola Ige. They were so referred because of their praetorian origin and not so subtle imposition. These parties held no authority of their own, no mind of their own and no identity of their own nor an ideology of their own. However, the sudden death of Abacha on June 8, 1998 marked the end of his transition program of self-succession, which ushered the Fourth Republic with General Abdulsalam Abubakar at the helm of affairs and who led a short and brief transition program. At the end of the usual alignment and re-alignment as well as mergers, 26 political associations sought for provisional registration but only nine parties were provisionally registered.

After the local government elections, three political parties out of the nine were fully registered to contest the elections. They are the People's Democratic Party (PDP), the All People's Party (APP) later known as the All Nigeria People's Party (ANPP) and the Alliance for Democracy (AD). Yet by May 29th 1999 when the democratic process was concluded with the emergence of the PDP government and General Olusegun Obasanjo as the Executive President of the Federation, the ethnic coloration of the past experiments still remained visible in the Nigerian national life most especially politics. The ANPP was considered to be a party predominantly occupied by the Hausa/Fulani and AD as a direct successor to Chief Obafemi Awolowo's Action Group and Unity Party of Nigeria and as a result dominated the six Yoruba speaking states of Lagos, Ekiti, Ogun, Ondo, Osun and Oyo states until 2003 when it lost all except Lagos to the ruling PDP. The ruling People's Democratic Party (PDP) was, however, seen to have deviated a bit from the usual ethnic-religious dominated party politics of the past with their membership and formation cutting across the clime of Nigeria, with the late Chief S.D Lar, a frontline Middle Belt leader as the pioneer chairman . The mission of the politicians in the PDP fold, apart from ousting the military was to show that the political class could cohere into one formidable force. However, if this was desirous at the time, it was soon to prove the incohesiveness of the PDP. For even as the political class verily cohered and presented a formidable front that wrestled power and became the dominant party in the country, the party became a collection and an amalgamation of strange bed fellows. The PDP was to witness a breakaway under the civilian administration of Chief Olusegun Obasanjo that was accused of scheming out many of the founding members of the party during a revalidation for members of which the then Vice President Atiku Abubakar was included, and also probably using an anti-corruption agency, the Economic and Financial Crimes Commission (EFCC) under Nuhu Ribadu to witch-hunt his perceived political opponents. Coupled with this is the self-styled do-or-die kind of politics that brought in the late President Umar Musa Yar'adua to power. However, the monster called ethnicity reared its ugly head again with the death of President Umaru Musa Yar'adua in view of the intrigues that preceded the processes of choosing a successor.

Some of the party's elders in the North claimed that at inception, the party held a gentleman's agreement to rotate power between the North and the South. Thus, Chief Olusegun Obasanjo, in serving the quota of the South, ruled for eight (8) years and while exiting the Aso Rock, installed Alhaji Umar Yar'adua in a process he called "do-or-die." Unfortunately, Yar'adua could not make it even to the end of the first tenure of his administration; he died in the third year as a result of ill health. Before his death, a lot of controversies and outcries especially from the Save Nigeria Group (SNG) convened by Pastor Tunde Bakare came up as a result of how the president's sickness was shrouded in mystery and the vacuum his absence had created. His Vice, Dr. Goodluck Jonathan, was eventually sworn in as Acting President to meet up with constitutional provision. He was later sworn in as substantive president following the confirmation of the death of his principal. He served in that capacity for over a year before the next round of general elections came up in April, 2011.

In the build up towards the general elections of April 2011, the Northern Political Forum (NPF) an ethnic forum, came up as a pressure group within the ruling PDP to demand that the gentleman agreement of the party prior to 1999 should be invoked. They argued that the late President Umaru Yar'adua from the North died after three years of the eight years that the North was supposed to be in power. Thus, their demand was for a Northerner to emerge as the flag bearer of the ruling People's Democratic Party.

To the utter chagrin of the Northern Elders, Dr. Goodluck Jonathan threw his cap in the ring owing largely to the calls from his fellow Ijaw people and other Niger Delta citizens who saw it as an opportunity for them being from the oil producing communities and minority ethnic group to produce Nigeria's elected president for the first time. His candidacy was also supported by Christians especially of the Middle Belt (North Central) stock, particularly Plateau, Benue, Taraba, Nassarawa, Kogi States, etc, who saw him as one that could help protect their interests and change what they saw as injustice to the rights of minorities.

In the intrigues that followed, the Northern Political Forum under the leadership of Alhaji Adamu Ciroma, set up a committee to support the three prominent contestants for the presidential ticket from the North, namely; General Ibrahim Babangida, Alhaji Atiku Abubakar and the former Governor of Kwara State, Dr.Olusola Saraki (now late), to look into the matter, compare notes and come up with the candidate who had the best political credentials to face the incumbent at the primaries.

Former Vice President Atiku Abubakar emerged as the candidate of the Northern Political Elite after votes were cast for the three, but he was later defeated by the incumbent President Goodluck Jonathan at the primaries. President Goodluck Jonathan emerged as the PDP flag bearer to face General Muhammadu Buhari (Rtd) of the

Congress for Progressive Change (CPC) and Mallam Nuhu Ribadu of the Action Congress of Nigeria (ACN), both Northerners in the April 2011 Presidential elections. President Goodluck Jonathan of the People's Democratic Party was returned as the winner in an announcement made by Prof. Attahiru Jega, Chairman of the Independent National Electoral Commission, INEC.

The runner-up of the presidential elections, Gen. Mohammadu Buhari, rejected the results of the polls and alleged rigging in the South-East and South-South parts of the country and proceeded to seek redress at the electoral tribunal. There were also attacks and gruesome killings of innocent citizens including National Youth Service Corps members in the Northern states of Bauchi and Kaduna who helped in conducting the polls. The activities of the self-acclaimed Boko-Haram Islamic sect, which had been in existence, took up a new dimension, and their killings continued almost unabated.

Amidst all these pandemonium, the North has been accused at different fora by the Southerners of holding on to power for more number of years both during civilian administrations and military regimes.

For the Northerners (those in the ruling People's Democratic Party), their agreement for power sharing started with the election of Gen. Olusegun Obasanjo in 1999, and they expected the party hierarchy to respect that agreement. But for other Nigerians outside the PDP, that agreement was seen as a party arrangement and not a constitutional provision. Therefore, to such individuals, other political parties, human rights' organizations, pressure groups and other non-governmental organizations, the most credible candidate should be the choice of all Nigerians.

Meanwhile, the Northern politicians are strategizing for a grand plan to wrest power from the incumbent. A courtesy call led by the late Chief Lar under the auspices of Middle Belt Elder's Forum promised to support President Goodluck if he decides to contest for the office of the president in 2015.

Peradventure, if Jonathan should contest for 2015 and win, it will increase discontent in the North and if he loses, there will also be discontent in the South-South and among other minorities of the Middle Belt. If this is not handled right, the seemingly ensuing crises could be bloodier. This could reverberate to other parts of the country and even trigger another secessionist move which will only cause an unimaginable loss of lives and property. The phenomenon of power tussle prevalent in the Nigerian political atmosphere is not healthy for the nation either. Ethnicity and religious bigotry have colored the political landscape for the mere fact that everybody is scrambling to grab as much of the national cake as possible for self, family members and cronies.

The emphasis is no longer about competent leadership, accountability and the common good of the citizenry. So much ethnic and religious sentiments are preferred by many while very few people talk about competence, accountability, strength of character to govern a heterogeneous people like Nigerians and incorruptibility, to set an example for others, and also a crystal clear vision to carry others along. However, now that Goodluck Jonathan is the President, and 2015 is still a long way to come, scheming has already started on how to wrestle power. In the pandemonium, there is a clear divide along ethnic lines as can be seen in the G7 Governors mostly from the north. The centre seems to be attracting everybody like the pull of gravity for the control of power and the resources that are massively vested at the centre.

CHAPTER TWO

RELIGIOUS BIGOTRY

Religious bigotry is another major threat to the corporate existence of Nigeria. Bigoted means having such a strong opinion about race, religion or politics, that one is not willing to listen to someone else's opinion.

The term 'bigotry' is also defined as bigoted behavior or beliefs, sensational news stories that just encourage bigotry and intolerance while a bigot is a person that engages in such a behavior or has such beliefs. Religion, on the other hand, is defined as one of the systems of faith that is based on the beliefs in the existence of a particular God or gods. The concept has also been defined as a particular interest or influence that is very important in one's life. In its own definition, the **Oxford Learner's Dictionary** explained religion as the belief in a super human controlling power that is entitled to obedience and worship. It goes further to state that it is a particular system of faith and worship that one is entitled to.

Religion is a body of truths, laws and rites by which man is subordinated to the transcendent being. This implies that religion deals with norms and rules that emanated from God and which must be followed by the believers. It is man's intuition of the sacred and ultimate reality and his expression of that awareness in concrete life.

Still, religion can be understood as a particular system or set of systems in which doctrines, myths, rituals, sentiments and other similar elements are inter-related. Or, it can be seen as a system of symbols which acts to establish powerful, persuasive and long lasting moods and motivations in men by formulating conceptions of a general order of existence and clothing these conceptions with such an aura of factuality that the moods and motivation seem uniquely realistic.

Religion can be understood in two ways; first in a material sense, it refers to religious establishment (that is institutions and officials) as well as to social groups and movements whose primary interests are found within religious concerns and secondly, in the spiritual sense which deals with models of social and individual behavior that help believers to organize their everyday lives. In this sense, religion has to do with the idea of transcendent, supernatural realities and the sacred; as a system of language and practice that organizes the world in terms of what is deemed holy and the ultimate conditions of existence.

Ideally, religion is supposed to be a medium through which humans relate with the Almighty God and the doctrines found in all religions should foster peaceful co-existence. Every religion in the world has as its guiding principles; the fact that we should do unto others what we want them to do unto us, although this is stated in different ways in the religious beliefs, the golden rule or the laws of the Karma as it is referred to variously.

Unfortunately, in Nigeria today, religious bigotry has affected the way the two most pronounced religious believers (Christians and Muslims) perceive each other, creating mutual suspicion and distrust and unsettling the pendulum of peace which has unleashed the nation into a theatre of massive killings mostly of innocent lives. Ethno-religious conflict which is a situation whereby the relationship between members of one ethnic or religious group and another of such group in a multi-ethnic and multi-religious society is characterized by lack of cordiality, mutual suspicion, fear and tendency towards violent confrontation has now become a recurring decimal in Nigeria.

In fact, this mutual suspicion and lack of cordiality among various ethnic components explain why ethno-religious conflicts have become recurring events in Nigeria, This started after independence in 1960, and today, many parts of Nigeria have become theatres of war characterized by ethnic and religious crises.

Notable ethno-religious crisis in the country include; the Maitatsine religious disturbances in parts of Kano and Maiduguri in the early 1980s, JimetaYola crisis/religious disturbances (1984), Zangon Kataf crisis in Kaduna State (1992), Bulunkutu Christian-Muslim skirmishes (1981-1982).

However, with the birth of the Fourth Republic, the spate of ethno-religious crises in Nigeria has increased, taking even more deadly dimensions. Within the last one and a half decade the first round of ethnic and religious riots in

Nigeria was in July, 1999, when some Oro-cultist in Shagamu in Ogun State accused a Hausa woman of coming out when the cultists were outside with their Gnome. This led to some altercations which eventually led to full blown crisis. Many people, majority of Hausa and Yoruba tribes, lost their lives. The infamy was, however, temporarily put to check only when a dusk to dawn curfew was imposed on the sleepy town of Shagamu.

Unfortunately, however, as the infamy was put off in Shagamu, reprisal started in Kano, a major Hausa city. As a result, many people died and property worth millions of naira destroyed. Kano residents of Southern extraction who had lived all their lives in the ancient city of Kano had to return to their native lands for safety and recount their losses. When Kano city was settling down for peace, Lagos erupted with another orgy of violence, visibly as a mark of vengeance of the Kano crisis and killing of the Yoruba tribesmen. This time, the Odua People's Congress (OPC) moved against the Hausa/Fulani traders in the popular mile 12 market and for two days, the area was turned to a killing field.

The recent and most recurring "ethno-religious" conflict is the Jos crisis, the capital of Plateau State. It has become the physical graveyard to hundreds of people including children cut down midstream in the insipid bloodletting now the lot of Jos and its environs. While the disturbances wear the toga of religious fanaticism in the Maitatsine days, its true color began to show with the current democratic dispensation. In 2004, the riots surged and virtually claimed hundreds of lives in southern part of Plateau; Langtang North, Wase and Shendam, leading to a declaration of state of emergency in 2004 during the tenure of the erstwhile Governor, Joshua Dariye.

Jos first experienced violent ethno-religious crisis on September 7, 2001, which shattered the innocence of Plateau State as a religiously tolerant state. In 2008, the November crisis evolved after state wide local government council elections. The crisis lasted for days, leaving in its trail, scores of lives and property destroyed. On Sunday, 17th January, 2010, Jos witnessed another ethno-religious conflict which was a consequence of religious intolerance and again, Jos was engulfed in a major orgy of killings, mayhem and wanton destruction of lives and property. The level of destruction assumed new dimensions in Bukuru particularly as houses were completely brought down to their foundation. Tensions spread to Bauchi, Kano, Kaduna, Nassarawa and Gombe States. State governments of Ondo, Oyo, Benue and Nasarawa sent buses to transport their students and other citizens to their home states. An imminent natural calamity became palpable.

However, the problem of ethno-religious crisis in Nigeria has proven to be unsolvable, because various measures taken against it proved to be either inadequate or ineffective in the sense that they were characterized by lack of sincerity and political will and have become even monotonous. Various panels and Judicial Commissions of Inquiry were set up to investigate the crisis, but none of the white papers released after such investigations had been implemented successfully. This is a proof of leadership failure in Nigeria.

Another dangerous dimension that fanned the embers of religious bigotry was during the build up to the general elections of April, 2011. In the campaigns that preceded the election, politicians and some clerics were at the forefront of campaigning for people that belonged to their religious groups to be elected into public offices. This is without recourse to the track records of such persons and their standing in terms of integrity and the strength of character to deliver the dividends of democracy to the masses. Both Christians and Muslims are guilty of bigotry in this instance. According to Christian awareness.org. in a publication on their website, "we are where we are today" because of leadership failure at all levels of governance, characterized by the military incursion into governance. Now, Nigerians have the chance to put their acts together and move the country forward by electing credible and honest people who in turn, are expected to provide the required leadership that will propel the nation to greatness.

Sadly, religious bigotry is being introduced into the polity by some desperate politicians who do not mean well for Nigerians and Nigeria as a nation. In as much as religion is pertinent to human beings, it is equally not in the best interest of the corporate existence of the nation to use it as a political tool, hence up till now, it has never guaranteed honesty, fairness, humility, kindness, courtesy, compassion and God-fearing leadership in Nigeria.

The election that was adjudged to be the fairest in the country which was annulled was a Muslim-Muslim ticket comprising the late Chief M. K. O. Abiola from the South and Alhaji Babagana Kingibe from the North. Nigerians came out *en masse* and defied for the first time the religious beliefs of both the Presidential candidate and his running mate, to vote for the duo that they believed could deliver to them the basic necessities of life. Unfortunately today, there is polarization and suspicion in the polity as a result of the resurgence of religious bigotry.

Nigerians are a highly religious people where you see Muslims observing piously, the five pillars of Islam and the Christians fellowshipping with others as they serve God, while the traditionalists are also committed in practicing their own religious belief.

Until the early 2000 when there was absolute peace and

mutual co-existence, Christians always shared Christmas rice and gifts with their Muslim neighbors who were always very happy to receive from them and also came out to watch as Christians dance in celebration of the birth of the Lord Jesus Christ. Likewise at every Sallah celebration, Christians looked forward to eating and sharing in the joy of their Muslim brothers who were always willing to share with the Christians. It was difficult to identify whether one person belonged to a particular religion and the other person to another until some selfish and greedy political jingoists in the quest for cheap power decided to fan the embers of religious discord in the polity. Suddenly, the peace, the harmony and the cordiality among the people began to give way to suspicion, distrust and hatred. Christians and Muslims no longer eat from the same plate due to mutual suspicion of each other. Neighbors suddenly became enemies to themselves to the extent that the person you shared food and excitement with yesterday is the same person that is hated with all passion and is seen as the enemy to be annihilated. What is even more disturbing is the fact that the people seem to be ignorant of the idea that the enemy is different; the enemy is that self-acclaimed hero who incites people at nocturnal meetings on the eve of elections by using cheap religious blackmail to win election.

Thus, religious bigotry became an effective tool in the hands of those who desire excessive power. Religious bigotry has never promoted peace, unity and progress. Therefore, proponents of such should know that it only unnecessarily heats up the polity and makes it ungovernable. What Nigeria needs at this critical moment is peaceful co-existence to enable her citizen's put their violent past behind them in order to face that bright future that lies ahead and to leave better legacies for the forth coming generation.

CHAPTER THREE

CORRUPTION

Another issue that has continued to persist and constitutes a major threat to the corporate existence of the Nigerian state is corruption. Corruption is endemic in most government agencies and parastatals and it is not peculiar to any continent, region or ethnic group. It cuts across faiths, religious denominations and political systems, and it affects young and old, men and women alike. Corruption is found in democratic and dictatorial politics as well as in feudal, capitalist and socialist economies. Christian, Muslim, Hindu and Buddhist cultures are equally bedeviled by corruption. And corrupt practices did not begin today; its history is as old as the world. Ancient civilizations have traces of wide spread illegality and corruption. Thus, corruption has been ambiguous in complex societies from ancient Egypt, Israel, Rome and Greece down to the present. The magnitude of corruption, however, differs from country to country as some are more corrupt than others. Since corruption is not new, and since it is a global phenomenon, it is not peculiar to Nigeria. However, corruption is pandemic in Nigeria, and has become the bane of the Nigerian people as most leaders and the followers are corrupt.

Corruption can be defined as a perversion or a change from good to bad. It involves the violation of established rules for personal gain and profit, as well as efforts to secure wealth or power through illegal means and private gain at public expense or misuse of public power for private benefits.

In addition, corruption is a behavior which deviates from the formal duties of a public role because of private gains regarding personal, close families, private clique, pecuniary or status gains. It is a behavior which violates rules against the exercise of certain types of duties for private gains regarding influence. This definition includes such behavior as bribery, (use of a reward to prevent the judgment of a person in a position of trust); nepotism, (bestowal of patronage by reason of ambition, relationship rather than result); and misappropriation (Illegal appropriation of public resources for private uses). Corruption is an anti-social behavior which contains the improper benefits contrary to legal and usual norms, and which undermine the authority to improve the living condition of the people.

Recent developments in Nigeria where discoveries of stolen public funds ran into billions of U.S Dollars and Nigerian Naira make these definitions very adequate and appropriate.

Corruption is probably the main means to accumulate quick wealth in Nigeria. Corruption occurs in many forms, and it has contributed immensely to the poverty and misery of a large segment of the Nigerian population.

Despite the fact that corruption can be found in all facets in the society and nations around the world, it is however a viable enterprise in the third world, especially Nigeria. The causes of corruption are myriad; and they have political and cultural variables.

Some facts point to a link between corruption and social diversity, ethno-linguistic fractionalization and the proportions of country's population adhering to different religious traditions. Studies by other scholars support the fact that corruption is widespread in most non-democratic countries, and particularly, in countries that have been branded neo-patrimonial, kleptocratic and prebendal. Thus, the political system and the culture of a society could make the citizens more prone to corrupt activities. However, the fundamental factors that engender corrupt practices in Nigeria include:

(1)   Great inequality in the distribution of wealth.

(2)   Political office as the primary means of gaining access to wealth.

(3)   Conflict between changing moral codes.

(4)   The weakness of social and governmental enforcement mechanism and

(5)   The absence of a strong sense of national community.

Greed and ostentatious life style are potential root causes of corruption. Some societies in love with ostentatious lifestyle may delve into corrupt practices to feed their lifestyle and also embrace a lifestyle of public sleaze and lack of decorum. The customs and attitudes of the society may also be contributing factors. Gift giving as an expression of loyalty or tributes to traditional rulers may be fabrics of the society but it equally has the tendency to corrupt or at other times, such gifts are in most cases given with the deliberate intention to corrupt.

Other causes of corruption in Nigeria today are:

(1)   Weak government institutions.

(2)   Poor pay incentives.

(3)   Lack of openness and transparency in public service.

(4)   Absence of effective political financing

(5)   Ineffective political processes.

(6)   Culture and acceptance of corruption by the populace.

(7)   Poverty

(8)   Ethnic and religious differences and

(9)   Resource scramble.

(10)   Over concentration and power at the center.

The causes of corruption in Nigeria cannot deviate significantly, if at all, from the above factors. However, obsession with materialism, compulsion for a short-cut to affluence, glorification and appropriation (of ill-gotten wealth) by the general public are among the reasons for the persistence of corruption in Nigeria. In addition to a diversity of ethnic nationalities, this is another hydra-headed monster that the Nigerian nation is contending with.

Corruption in Nigeria has taken up a certain nature, and the characteristics include; political corruption which takes place at the highest levels of political authority. It occurs when the politicians and the political decision-makers, who are entitled to formulate, establish and implement the laws in the name of the people, are themselves corrupt. Policy formulation and legislation are probably tailored to benefit politicians and legislators. This is classified as both corruption and greed as it affects the manner in which decisions are made; it manipulates political institutions, rules of procedure, and distorts the institutions of government. Bureaucratic corruption occurs in the public administration or the implementation end of politics. Bureaucratic corruption is low level and is encountered daily at places like the hospitals, schools, local licensing offices, police and taxing offices, etc. This is a corruption of need as a result of poor welfare package, and it occurs when one obtains a business from the public sector through inappropriate procedure.

Electoral corruption has become rampant in Nigeria where votes are bought, people are killed or maimed in the name of election, losers end up as winners in elections, and votes turned up in areas where votes were not cast. Corruption in office involves sale of legislative votes, administrative or judicial decisions or governmental appointment. Disguised payment in the form of gifts, legal fees, employment, favors to relatives, social influence and other relationship that sacrifices the public interest and welfare, with or without the implied payment of money, has become the order of the day. Other forms of corruption in practice today in Nigeria include;

(a)   **Bribery:** This is the payment in money or kind, which is taken or given in a corrupt relationship. These include kickbacks, gratification, pay-off, sweeteners, greasing palms, etc.

(b)   **Fraud**: This involves some kind of trickery, swindle and deceit, counterfeiting, racketing, smuggling and forgery.

(c) **Embezzlement**: This is theft of public resources by public officials. It is when a public official steals from the public institution in which he/she is employed. In Nigeria, the embezzlement of public funds is one of the most common ways of economic accumulation, perhaps due to lack of strict regulatory systems.

(d) **Extortion:** This is money and other resources extracted by the use of coercion, violence or threats to use force. It is often seen as extraction from below. The Nigerian Police and the Customs Officers are probably the main culprits in Nigeria.

(e) **Favoritism:** This is a mechanism of power abuse implying a highly biased distribution of state resources. This is usually done to favor friends, family and anybody close to one.

(f) **Nepotism:** This is a special form of favoritism in which an office holder prefers his/her kinfolk and family members. Nepotism occurs when one is exempted from the application of certain laws or regulations or given undue preference in the allocation of scarce resources. Below is a list containing the names of institutions perceived as the most corrupt according to the Nigeria Survey on Corruption report of June 2003 from the Institute for Development Research, Ahmadu Bello University, Zaria (IDR Zaria).

1.   Nigerian Police

2.   Political parties

3.   National and State Assemblies

4.   Local and Municipal Governments.

5.   Federal and State Executive Councils

6.   Traffic Police and FRSC

7.   PHCN

However, there were certain measures taken by various administrations to tackle the menace of corrupt practices in the polity but the fight turned out to be a failure as a result of the following reasons:

(1)   Insincerity of government

(2)   Pre-bargaining and negotiation

(3)   Low deterrent-strengthen punitive measures.

(4)   Lack of virile and political social movement to tackle corruption.

(5)   Insecurity of informants.

(6)   Low public participation in government

(7)   Corrupt electoral system.

(8)   Nepotism.

(9)   Weak government institutions.

(10)   Systemic disorder.

At independence, precisely during the First Republic when true federalism was in practice, corruption was kept at a manageable level. Azikiwe was alleged to be the first major political figure investigated for questionable practices. It was said that in 1944, a firm belonging to Azikiwe and family bought a bank in Lagos. The bank was said to be procured to strengthen local control of the financial industry. Albeit, a report about transactions carried out by the bank showed that though Azikiwe had resigned as chairman of the bank, the chairman as at the time of the investigation was an agent of his. The report came up with the findings that most of the paid up capital of the African Continental Bank was from the Eastern Regional Financial Corporation.

In Western Nigeria, a politician, Adegoke Adelabu, was allegedly investigated following charges of political corruption leveled against him by the opposition. The report led to the demand for his resignation as district council head. In 1962, Chief Obafemi Awolowo was said to have been indicted and a Coker Commission of Enquiry which was set up, found that a substantial amount of money was misappropriated from the coffers of the Western Regional Government.

In the Northern Region, against the backdrop of corruption allegation leveled against some native authority officials in Bornu, the Northern Government enacted laws to forestall any further breach of regulations. Later, it was the British administration that was accused of corrupt practices following the results of elections which enthroned a Fulani political leadership in Kano and later reports linking the British authorities to electoral irregularities were discovered. However, since the military takeover, and the introduction of unitary as a form of government and the subsequent discovery of crude oil, corruption took on a new look and started growing in leaps and bounds. Corruption became a way of life and the military regimes that came up as an intervention force could not bring the monster of corruption to its knees. In fact, some of the military regimes were more corrupt than the civilian administrations. The administration of General Buhari (Rtd) in 1985 convicted a cross section of political gladiators for different corrupt practices before the administration was terminated in the same year.

Since the return to civil rule in 1999, corruption and corrupt practices have continued to be embraced by political office holders today to the extent that billions of Nigerian Naira and dollars were found to be looted and linked to the names of Ex-Governors, Federal and State Legislators, ministers, etc. by the Economic and Financial Crimes Commission (E.F.C.C) but the courts of law have not been able to prosecute all the perpetrators. Instead most of them are being celebrated and reelected into political offices.

A current reality of corruption was recently made public when billions of naira was discovered to have been paid to oil marketers as subsidies for petroleum products, but some of them actually diverted the funds.

Corruption has eaten deep into the fabric of society which has resulted to the prevalence of hunger and starvation. A large chunk of Nigeria's national resources are being depleted by pilfering and negligence, for example, in the extractive industry, through bunkering and oil theft, and in the public and private sectors through losses of revenue and corruption.

Nigeria is where she is today because of corruption and greed which is prevalent in government circles in the sense that a tiny percentage of the population pilfer or embezzle public funds that are meant to provide general infrastructure to cater for the needs of the people.

Instead of abating, the situation continues to persist, thus increasing the general discontent among the lower class, heightening the level of apprehension. In recent times, Nigerians woke up to hear that a serving minister bought two armored cars for 255 million naira to the utter dismay of Government and public despair. If left unchecked, it is certain that the economy of the nation will crumble. This may result to a general uprising by the under privileged class as evident in some of the Arab countries.

CHAPTER FOUR

ECONOMIC DEPRIVATION

Another factor that may constitute a threat to the corporate existence of Nigeria beyond 2015 as one viable entity is the scourge of economic deprivation. This is another area of neglect that has resulted in Nigerians going through untold hardships.

According to the **Oxford Advanced Learners' Dictionary of English Language**, deprivation means *"something you need or usually have that you are prevented from having."* It can also be defined as *"a lack of something that you need or want."* Thus, economic deprivation can be defined as a situation in which a person lacks the necessary (monetary) resources to live at the same level of those around him or her.

Economic deprivation in the context of this write up could be seen as the inability of government to provide the basic necessities of the citizenry which include food, water, shelter, healthcare, roads, quality education, provision of gainful employment and security of lives and property of its citizens.

The reason for the persistence of deprivation despite the abundance of oil wealth, diverse mineral resources and vast arable land for agricultural production is the kind of federalism that is practiced in Nigeria today which is more of a "centralized military garrison.

Prior to the military incursion into politics in Nigeria, the country was practicing real federalism based on regions whereby the three regions of Northern, western and Eastern Nigeria controlled their own resources. Each region operated independently without undue interference and hindrance from the centre. This system provided dynamism in economic development. The reason is that they mobilized their human and material resources in revenue generation. Each region identified its area of strength and developed a plan of human capacity building, which resulted in a high pool of intellectual resource contribution and a highly skilled national strength.

Under our founding fathers, the regions experienced

massive infrastructural facelift, excellent facilities and enviable macro and micro-economic policies. They generated their revenue independently which was ploughed back in developing their regional economies. This system gave everybody a sense of duty and belonging. There was willingness on the part of the people in each region to contribute to their regional economies because they trusted their leaders to use the proceeds gotten from their common wealth to cater for the needs of the citizens. Therefore, nobody was deprived because deprivation in this sense would have meant that the people deprived themselves because they refused to explore the wealth available to them. This period marked true federalism in display.

However, with the military incursion into politics and their having access to power in Nigeria, the productive and result-oriented regional structure of government was replaced with a centralized structure. With this new development, the control of all resources was hijacked to the centre. This was made possible by various military decrees and acts that gave the federal government total ownership and control of all resources.

For example, the Land Use Act of 1978 (1993) gave the state governments absolute ownership and control over land and the resources found therein.

The general principles of the act states that; subject to the provisions of this decree, all lands comprised in the territory of each state in the federation are hereby vested in the military Governor of the state and such land shall be held in trust and administered for the use and common benefit of all Nigerians.

By this provision, the act altered existing land laws (particularly in the Southern part of the country) in three fundamental ways; (1) It removed corporate groups, families and chiefs from the trusteeship of land and replaced them with the state Governor; (2) Individual interest in land which has expanded with economic development arising from the oil boom is now one of occupancy and therefore falls short of the communities alloyed interest in land which is now denied or frozen: and (3) the act destroyed local sovereignties and merged them into a single sourcing.

Part 1 Section II states that "as from the commencement of this Act:

(a)   All land in urban areas shall be under the control and management of the Governor of each state; and

(b)   All other land shall, subject to this act, be under the control and management of the local government within the area of jurisdiction of which the land is situated.

However, two radical changes flowed from part 1 of the act. The legal status of the Nigerian land user becomes that of statutory occupancy, not one of ownership; and the economic interest and benefits of statutory rights of occupancy are securely limited by law since claims are restricted to improvements made on the land.

The act stated that while urban lands were placed under the control and management of the Governor of the state with a "Land Use Committee" as an advisory body, on the other hand, other lands were placed under the control and management of the Local Government in which the land is situated with the "Land Allocation Advisory Committee." Land Use Act; The land under the control of Local Government which is termed as "Other Land" is meant to be used for agricultural production, but because of oil boom, all these have been abandoned while all local councils await monthly handouts from the federal account.

Secondly, the Petroleum Act of 1969 (1991) gave the Federal Government absolute powers of control over all petroleum resources within the borders of the country. In the Petroleum Act of 1961 Part 1 Section 1: States that:

(1)   "The ownership and control of all petroleum in, under or upon in any lands to   which this section applies shall be vested in the state.

(2)   This section applies to all land (including land covered by water) which:

(3)   Is in Nigeria.

(4)   Is under the territorial waters of Nigeria; or

(5)   Forms part of the continental shelf; or

(6)   Forms part of the Exclusive Economic zone of Nigeria.

(7)   In this section, references to territorial waters are references to the expression as defined in the territorial waters act.

Another area of neglect is the mining sector where different types of mineral resources are discovered to be in existence, but they have largely been left untapped or at the mercy of illegal miners. Mineral resources abound in all states of the federation but ownership and control of mineral are vested in the state (Minerals and Mining Act 2007).It states that "The entire property in and control of all mineral resources in under or upon land in Nigeria, its contiguous continental shelf and all rivers, streams and water courses throughout Nigeria, any area covered by its territorial waters or constituency and the exclusive economic zone is and shall be vested in the Government of the Federation for and on behalf of the people.

Thirdly, the National Waterways Decree of 1997 that conceded all rights of having access to all waterways in the country for whatever purpose to the Federal Government of Nigeria, etc. This system has been continued even now that power has since returned to civilians from the military. The Federal Government has totally abandoned every other productive sector of the economy and solely depends on petroleum and petroleum products which constitute about 95% of the export commodities of the economy, as at 2011. Cocoa and rubber make up for a meager 5% of export commodities as at 2011, while Industrial production growth is put at 1.8% (2011).

As the population continued to grow and the neglect on the part of the government persisted, the rate of unemployment also kept rising. Presently, it rates about 21%, this is also considering the fact that hundreds of thousands of students graduate from universities, polytechnics and colleges of education with no gainful employment.

As a result of the deprivations, hunger and starvation keep persisting and growing at an alarming rate. The Central Intelligence Agency (CIA) World Fact Book 2007 still put the estimated percentage of people in Nigeria living below the poverty line of one dollar per day at an incredible 70%.

Statistics gotten from Nigeriaworld.com reveal that the oil industry employs about ten thousand (10,000) people out of population of over 130 million Nigerians. It also shows that 1% of the population controls oil wealth accruing from oil sales.

An illustration from the Prisons Fellowship of Nigeria describes the damage at which socio-economic deprivation has done to the Nigerian society. It avers that "marginalization, poverty, socio-economic deprivations are largely synonymous with crime, criminality, court overload and prison congestion.

Our prisons are populated by inmates largely bedeviled by poverty and socio-economic deprivations. Homeless street children turned thieves, thugs, rubbers, drug pushers and prostitutes and if they are caught, they can neither hire a lawyer nor afford court fines. They are dumped in prison to sulk and strategize, while bemoaning their sojourn behind the grey walls and journey through the dark harrowing tunnel.

When they manage to get discharged, they face a harder life sentence, hostile and indiscriminate legislation, sanctimonious social reception; what becomes evident is high rate of recidivism, escalation in sophistication and rate of crime, fear and insecurity." That is exactly the aftermath of economic deprivation in Nigeria today: Fear and Insecurity.

Another dimension to deprivation that constitutes a threat to the continuous existence of the country is the inevitable fact that democracy as currently practiced in Nigeria is too expensive to be maintained. In fact, the maintenance of Nigeria's nascent democracy has continued to be at the detriment of majority of Nigerians. Political office holders enjoy attractive allowances and other juicy perks of office that are taking away a chunk of the resources which could have been used for other meaningful developmental projects to better the lives of the common people.

A recent report by the business day research unit titled "Budget 2013: Facts behind the figures" shows and further reinforces the general perception that Nigeria's cost of governance is on the high side and is unwieldy. In comparing the budgetary allocation between Nigeria and South Africa, the report shows that the National Assembly's $995 million (N150 billion equivalent) allocation as proposed in the 2013 budget awaiting President Goodluck Jonathan's assent, is approximately 6.4 times higher than the U.S155 million (N24 billion) allocation made to the South African parliament in its 2012/2013 budget.

On a per capita basis (head) basis, the allocation to the National Assembly translates to approximately US$2 million (N312 million) budget spent on each of the 468 members (360 members of the House or Representatives and 109 senators).

The N312 million budget spent per head for the Nigerian National Assembly is 6.4 times higher than the approximately N49 million (US$316,326) per head incurred on the 490 members (400 members of the House of Assembly and 90 members of the National Council of Provinces) of the South African parliament. According to the report, South Africa's budget spent on its parliament is lower, despite the country's US$113 billion equivalent 2012/2013 budget which is approximately 3.5 times higher than Nigeria's US$32 billion equivalent 2013 budget.

The implication is that as a proportion of the total budget, the National Assembly consumes approximately 3.02 percent of Nigeria's budget, compared to the 0.14 per cent consumed by the South African parliament. Thus, the Nigerian parliament budget consumption is 22 times higher than its South African counterpart, the business day report shows.

The report also indicates that the Nigerian presidency is also more expensive to maintain than the South Africa's presidency. It shows that Nigeria spends almost twice more money on its presidency than that of South-Africa. For the proposed 2013 budget, the allocation of N3b billion (US$228 million) to be consumed by the Nigerian presidency is approximately twice the US$119 million (N19 billion) allocation to the presidency in South Africa.

As a proportion of the budget, the allocation to the presidency in Nigeria is approximately 0.70 percent of Nigeria's budget, compared to South Africa's 0.11 percent of its budget, indicating that Nigeria's presidency consumes about seven times more of its national budget than South Africa's presidency.

As a top competitor for Foreign Direct Investment (FDI) in sub-Sahara Africa, analysts have often warned that the cost of governance in Nigeria is unnecessarily high, and may be eating away at the critical expenditure on infrastructure. If this high cost is not checked, they warn, it may affect Nigeria's long term competitiveness.

These are indications that the great majority of the citizens suffer deprivation by a very few privileged ones who happen to be in control of the resources accruing to the nation.

It would be recalled how in 2010 the Nigerian Labour Congress (NLC) and other Trade Unions organized mass rallies across the states of the federation to compel the Federal and States Governments to pay the sum of fifty three thousand naira N53,000.00 as minimum wage to all workers. After a long drawn battle, government and labour agreed on the paltry sum of eighteen thousand naira (N18, 000.00).

Most Nigerians hardly survive on this amount considering the fact that fuel price was jerked up from sixty-five naira (N65.00) per liter to ninety seven naira (N97.00) per liter and as a consequence, the prices of all other goods and services simultaneously went up. According to a report by Nigeria Intel; burden of recurrent expenditure : "lifestyle" March 31 2013,official figures from National Bureau of Statistics(NBS) indicate that 18 trillion naira in recurrent expenditure-operations, wages, salaries, purchase of goods and services as well as subsidies, among others in sharp contrast to 6.5 trillion naira spent on infrastructure between 1999-2011.The system obviously has been running in a rat race, tactically avoiding the way of emancipation which is the way to go.

CHAPTER FIVE
INSECURITY

Nigeria gradually slipped into the present level of insecurity over the years. Insecurity in Nigeria presently is a culmination of all the preceding threats to the corporate existence of the country.

Security is the basic condition to safety from harm and deprivation. It is applicable to persons, living things, an entity and inanimate objects. Thus, insecurity can be said to be the exposure to harm and the subjection to deprivation.

The Longman Dictionary of Contemporary English defines insecurity as a building or structure that is insecure and not safe, because it is likely to fall down. This clearly depicts the true picture of Nigeria today. Insecurity has torn the various regions or sections of the nation apart.

The Genesis

The aftermath of corruption, which is the looting of the resources meant for the general good of Nigerians, the polarization of ethnicity that breeds suspicion and distrust, religious bigotry that promotes the superiority of one religious belief over the other, and economic deprivation that deprives Nigerians of having access to the natural resources in abundance in the land, all contributed immensely to the general insecurity that is being experienced in the country today.

Despite constant stress, it would seem the functions of convergence of interest are working all over the country, albeit unguided. Nonetheless, the factors of divergence continue to nibble at the roots of stability and survival. Such factors include the high level of polarization among the elite, the lack of unity among various ethnic groups and the lack of concurrence within the polity on where the country should be headed or what her aspiration should be.

The country called Nigeria is a creation of the British and the process of state formation ended with the British era of colonization. However, because the British amalgamated diverse groups of people into one nation, the attainment of independence brought a lot of conflicts in its wake. The struggle to control the state by different forces was informed by the need to appropriate resources. Therefore, the interest of all contending forces was for their communities and not for the emerging Nigerian state.

Thus, the issue of unrest developed, incomplete state formation and border adjustment, enforced union during colonial rule, mismanaged unity in pre and post-independence eras and poor governance heightening abject poverty and unleashing conflicts ripen the scene for permanent insecurity.

Most restraints to conflict, such as the family, religious teachings, moral and civil norms, weakened or collapsed against the growing child that is Nigeria. It was at this point that the military entered the fray believing that the crises of law and order required militarized regimentation and discipline to prevent the disintegration of the country.

It is unfortunate that the military could not arrest the situation but ended up complicating matters because military rule probably mismanaged the state, perverted and centralized institutions, entrenched corruption and instituted a conception of security that dehumanizes the human being.

The everyday insecurity confronting Nigerians is beyond the comprehension of the military. It stems from the unsatisfactory and unhealthy food they consume; the poorly staffed and equipped hospitals available; inability to pay for medication which can only function with a healthy diet, the unhealthy and confidence sapping clothes they wear, the resentment breeding schools they attend with classes under trees or in dilapidated buildings, to ill-motivated teachers who are constantly searching for greener pastures, school children turned into farm laborers, ill-equipped and ill-motivated secondary and tertiary education, poor and   non-existing transport infrastructure, inadequate public housing scheme, insufficient infrastructure like pipe borne water, electricity, sewage , drainage   and sanitation, irregular payment of salary and insecurity provided by the dozen ill motivated and brutalized security outfits. This variant of insecurity is beyond the comprehension of the military or the political class it mentored. Indeed, the military and political classes have used all means at their disposal to distance themselves from their fellow citizens' daily ordeal because they now feel threatened and therefore act to fortify their personal security.

These ugly situations have continued in a vicious circle to the extent that insecurity is threatening to tear the nation apart. This is all because the fundamental issues that could help stem this tide have been largely ignored by the leadership class. However, negligence has led to the following realities of insecurity in the country.

CURRENT SECURITY CHALLENGES

The Boko Haram Insurgency

The most vicious and dangerous dimension to the heightening state of insecurity is the one posed by the emergence of a group known in local parlance as BOKO HARAM which has been unleashing terror in the northern parts of the country. The term Boko Haram translated into Hausa language means "Western education is prohibited"

The *Jama'atuAhi As-Sunnah Li-Da'awatiWal-Jihad"*
(JASDJ) commonly known as Boko Haram or the *Nigerian Taliban* is a faction of the Sunni Islamic sect agitating for jihad. It is basically a Nigerian based group that seeks to overthrow the current democratic government to replace it with a form of Theocratic system of government that is based on Islamic sharia law.

It is a group that is said to comprise of "people committed to the propagation of the Prophet's teachings and jihad."

The sect was founded in early 2000 by a Muslim cleric, Mohammed Yusuf which gained a steady following in Maiduguri as it preached against secular values. It was claimed that he was later killed by Nigerian security forces in 2009 but his support base was sustained through the provision of meals and economic schemes including a youth empowerment program. He was also known for arranging cheap marriages for sect members.

Some analysts have ascribed the groups' growth to the provision of economic and social support by Boko Haram. The sect started using violence against government and police in 2003 while the first large attacks came in Bauchi and Maiduguri in July 2009 with more than 700 people killed in a five day uprising.

With the death of its leader, instead of abating, the group became Increasingly Sophisticated in its operations. In July 2010, Boko Harams' former second in command, AbubakarShekau, appeared in a video claiming leadership of the group and threatening attacks on western interest in Nigeria. Under his leadership which is in solidarity with the Al Qaeda and issuing threats to the United States, the group has continued to demonstrate growing operational capabilities, with an increased use of improvised explosive device [IED] attacks against soft targets.

The group also went ahead to release hundreds of prisoners from the Bauchi prisons in 2010 and also launched bombings in Jos and the New Year Eve bombing in the FCT Abuja. On 26 August 2011, the sect carried out its first attack on western interest by bombing the UN headquarters in Abuja that left 23 people dead while over 80 of the inhabitants were left with various degrees of injuries. While accepting responsibility for the attacks, the sect promised further attacks on US and Nigerian

Government interests.

Activities of the Boko Haram sect, which have spread over almost all the states in the north, have continued to pose a very serious security challenge, constituting a major threat to lives and property.

Owing largely to the weak security apparatus, poorly trained and ill-motivated personnel, the sect has been emboldened and has on a continuous basis carried out its activities undeterred. This resulted in fear and apprehension across the land. These attacks are mostly carried out on Christians and their places of worship thereby engendering a culture of mutual suspicion between the two religious groups not only in the north, but in the south also; every northerner is treated with suspicion.

Another set of people that have been affected by the Boko Haram onslaught are the Igbo people who are known to own business interests in all parts of the nation including the north. Most of them lost either business interests or their homes and a lot of them have already started migrating back to the east in their numbers.

The governors of the eastern states have met to discuss the fate of the Igbos living in the northern parts of the country as the activity of the sect continues almost unhindered. These acts have continued to generate a lot of debate about the workability of a strong united and virile Nigeria.

Militancy

Militant groups especially in the Niger Delta region of Nigeria in the recent past have unleashed untold terror in that part of the country all in a bid to draw the attention of government to the magnitude of environmental degradation caused by exploration activities and negligence and also to demand control of their natural resources which accounts for over 80% of Nigeria's earning. These militants brandished such sophisticated weapons that turned the area into an insecure zone. In their determination to achieve this, the Niger Delta militants went to the extent of attacking major multinational oil companies in the region, breaking pipelines to halt production of petroleum products. This led to a drastic drop in oil production which became a major concern to the Government of the day.

Despite the fact that the late President Umar Yar'adua granted amnesty to the militants and their subsequent rehabilitation, some of them like a faction of MEND (Movement for the Emancipation of Niger Delta) still remain in the creeks and this also constitutes insecurity considering the fact that it was not all the weapons that were submitted to government during the amnesty process.

'INDIGENE' VERSUS 'SETTLERS' CONFLICTS

Emphasis on ancestry and place of origin lead to observations such as the description of fellow Nigerians as indigene or settlers by local authorities. The rights and expectations of these citizens in that part of the country are governed by their classifications. In some states, indigenes pay less school fees than non-indigenes, a case of being a foreigner in one's own country. Those affected have developed a sense of alienation and discrimination.

To some Nigerians, the crisis of identity is real. Who really is a Nigerian? Is he defined by place of birth, color of skin or ancestry? Some Nigerians with Caucasian or Asiatic features find it difficult to convince others that they are indeed Nigerians since they are not black. Effective security depends on citizens' commitment. Commitment will be superficial where persons have doubt about who they are, whether they want to identify truly with the country and promote her security and survival. The indigene-settler conflicts are the basic cause of permanent insecurity in most of the Nigerian communities.

ARMED ROBBERY AND KIDNAPPING

The aftermath of corruption and economic deprivation is the prevalence of hunger and starvation arising mostly from unemployment and indolence. As a result of these, armed robbery and kidnapping have become common features in all parts of the country. This is in a bid for the hungry and starving unemployed youths to earn an illegal means of living. The sophistication with which these acts are carried out only leaves one wondering why such talents could be neglected and allowed to venture into a negative enterprise as such. Universally, criminals use technology and specialists knowledge to commit crimes.

Nigerian criminals, by their ingenuity, have beaten most law enforcement measures in the world to perpetuate credit card and bank frauds. They resort to crime because of lack of opportunities or the under-employment of talent. Some have wondered where Nigeria could be in terms of development, if only the ingenuity exhibited by some of the citizens in perpetuating crimes can be channeled into positive endeavor.

Road Mishaps and Air Disasters

As a result of the poor and non-existing transport infrastructure, Nigerians have suffered untold hardship when plying the roads. A lot of lives have been lost in road accidents and a lot more in plane crashes as a result of the corruption that prevails and poor management of the aviation sector. The transportation sector no longer guarantees the safety of lives and property thus constituting another area of insecurity.

In the road transport sector, examples of the major routes which have become death traps include the Benin-Ore road, the Lagos-Ibadan Express-Way, the Abuja-Lokoja road and the East –West road, amongst others. Hundreds of lives have been lost on these routes arising from auto crashes mostly due to the bad nature of the roads neglected by Government.

The aviation sector which is thought to provide succor against the backdrop of multiplicity and frequency of road mishaps, is also in a state of decadence. The rate of air disasters in Nigeria has risen to an alarming rate, thus the security of lives can no longer be guaranteed in that sector.

In May 2002, there was a plane crash in Kano with 75 people on board. Another incident occurred in Lagos on 22 October, 2005, having 116 people on board. The same year on 10th December, a jet crashed and burst into flames with 100 passengers on board that all lost their lives.

On October 29th 2006, a Boeing 737 plane crashed after takeoff from the Abuja airport, 104 people died including the then Sultan of Sokoto, Alhaji Adamu Maccido.

On June 3rd 2012, a Dana plane carrying 162 passengers crashed into a building in Lagos state, without a single survivor. The same year on December 15th, a military helicopter carrying the late former National Security Adviser, General Patrick Owoye Aziza and the late Governor of Kaduna state, Mr. Patrick Yakowa, crashed into the bush, killing all its occupants. The Taraba state Governor, Mr Danbaba Suntai is still recuperating from a chopper accident he was piloting himself.

Another plane crash occurred on October 3rd 2013 shortly after take-off from the Lagos international airport with 20 people on board including the corpse of the former Governor of Ondo State, Dr.Olusegun Agagu. 17 people died on that day.

All these have generated a lot of debate and have put a lot of unanswered questions on the ability of the aviation sector to secure lives of the people.

UNDER FUNDED POLICE FORCE

Six policing functions have been listed in Chapter19 of the Police Act of the laws of the federation and they are;

1. Crime prevention.

2. Detection and apprehension of offenders.

3. Preservation of law and order.

4. Protection of life and property.

5. Enforcement of all laws and regulations enacted by the federal, state and local governments.

6. Performance of such military duties within or outside Nigeria, when sanctioned by law.

It is expected that the police should be well funded to be able to carry out the above, but to the consternation of many, the Nigerian Police Force has been grossly underfunded. The Force is the largest single public sector organization in Nigeria. In 2008, it employed about 380,000 officers and other ranks to work in every nook and cranny of the country. The UN recommends that every nation should have a police officer for every 400,000 citizens. This is one of few global standards that Nigeria has nearly attained. It is expected that police officers should possess adequate level of education, training, kitting, technical competence and operational capacity to discharge their lawful functions. There is very little debate whether they (police) possess these. It is abundantly clear that they do not possess and this has continued to incapacitate their operational capability.

The Inspector General of Police, M.D ABUBAKAR in his maiden address to senior police officers in the country said that *"The police force has fallen to its lowest level; police duties have become commercialized and provided at the whims and caprices of the highest bidder..."*

The police stations, state Criminal Investigations Department and other operations offices have probably become business centers and collection points for rendering returns from all kinds of squads and teams set up for the benefit of superior officers. It is the opinion of some that special anti-robbery squads (SARS) have become killer teams engaging in shady operations for land speculators and debt collectors. Toll stations in the name of check points adorn the highways with policemen shamefully collecting money from motorists in full glare of the public.

It is also opined that police connive with suspects to turn against complainants and investigations are usually not conducted unless those involved pay money to the police. Justice has been perverted, people's rights denied, innocent souls committed to prison, torture and extra judicial killings perpetrated and so many people arbitrarily detained in the cells because they cannot afford the illegal bail monies being demanded.

Illegalities thrive under the watchful eyes of helpless by-standers because they have compromised the very ethics of their profession. The police force has probably lost its prestige because some members of the Nigerian public no longer have the slightest confidence in the ability of the Police to do any good thing."

It is worthy to note that the operational incapability of the police is at the detriment of the security of lives and property of the Nigerian citizenry.

The table below provides a comparative picture of budgetary allocation to the Nigerian police with about 400,000 men and the Nigerian military with about 76,000 which depicts the degree of underfunding of the police force.

Year	Military	Police
2013	364 billion	320 billion
2012	326.4 billion	331.2billion
2011	311.7 billion	304.7 billion
2010	231.9 billion	216 billion
2009	223 billion	195 billion

SOURCE: www.budgetoffice.org

The police formations and commands' budget for 2012 consisted of #290.7 billion for the personnel cost of between 380,000 and 400,000 police officers. The overhead cost of running 1,115 police divisions, 5,515 police stations and 5,000 police posts nationwide is a mere #8.1 bn. If the police divisions, stations and posts as bases are harmonized for equal overheads distribution, this sums up to about N696, 000 annually per division, station and post-even with zero amount going to headquarters, zonal and area commands. This is less than #200 per day to run a police station which explains why the police stations have no crime diary and even biro to take down statements.

The police is not expected to perform magic in the fight against crime and criminality, which is why the IGP M.DAbubakar insisted on Channels Television concerning police efforts that;

"We do so much with so little, even with nothing. This is the only country in the world where you go to the police station and there is no water, there is no light, there is no vehicle, there is no communication, and the police are expected to perform miracles. How do you do that? I don't know any other country, if you do please tell me. This is the only country in the world that you see a policeman on the street fighting robbers, fighting terrorists without bullet proof jackets, working in the rain without rain coats, and he still stays there."

POROUS BORDERS

Another area of concern that has heightened insecurity and fear is the porous nature of Nigeria's national borders. This has warranted the infiltration of dissident foreigners, illicit drugs and dangerous arms and ammunitions that pose serious threats to the security of lives and property. This is no thanks to the inefficiency of the ill-equipped and ill-motivated Nigerian Custom

Service, the Nigerian Immigration Service and the Nigerian Police Force. There has also been alleged high level of compromise in the force as criminals can connive with officers to carry out their nefarious activities. A typical example of the ill equipped nature of the police force was the explosion of a bomb under the nose of the Inspector General of Police at the Louis Edet House, Headquarters of the force.

In Nigeria, politics is militarized and violence is used as an electoral tool, leading to the inculcation of a culture ofviolence in society. Armed groups are not a new phenomenon. However, today's armed groups are better armed, better trained and increasingly sophisticated in their actions. Armed groups, hired by politicians, have now developed their own economic bases thereby saving themselves from their political patrons. This has led some groups to engage in the political process themselves.

Armed violence is about access to resources, whetherthrough committing crimes, playing on communal tension, stealing oil or winning elections. These are mostly encouraged by the do- or- die kind of politics that introduces the use of arms and ammunition to secure votes into political offices. Without addressing the key issues of resource control and distribution, armed violence is likely to continue unabated.

However, the spate of killings and the attendant atmosphere of insecurity in its wake have presented another opportunity to all true democrats who mean well for the corporate existence of the nation to come together and brainstorm so as to proffer solutions to the quagmire the country has found itself.

CHAPTER SIX

FOREIGN INTERFERENCE

While the country continues to groan under the yoke of ethnicity, religious bigotry, corruption, economic deprivation and insecurity that are threatening to tear the nation apart, an unseen but dangerous enigma that has been hovering within the vicinity of the Nigerian nation which is eating deep into the Nigerian nationhood revolves around the issue of subtle foreign interference. Most of the woes bedeviling Nigeria today are as a result of this western domination over the years that are still taking their toll on every aspect of our national life. The western domination of Nigeria and Africa as a whole is in three stages (phases) namely (1) Slavery and slave trade (2) Colonialism and (3) Neo-colonialism.

SLAVERY AND SLAVE TRADE

As a result of the growing sugar-cane and cotton plantations in Europe and America in the 17th to 18th centuries, there was need for more workforces to meet up with increasing demand due to the lack of industrialization at the time. Africans being black and physically strong became the target of the West for a ready workforce on their plantations. The Portuguese first experimented on the use of Africans on their plantations and when they discovered that the Negro (black man) could withstand the rigorous demands of farm work, they started coming to Africa to buy slaves from the African chiefs for onward shipment to their plantations.

It was soon discovered all over Europe and America that the black slaves were more productive, so a mad rush started all in a bid to purchase Africans for slavery abroad. Some of these westerners even went to the extent of instigating inter-tribal wars through the African chiefs whereby all the war captives readily became potential slaves for the Europeans. Slave trade thus became a major preoccupation in Africa and slavery was boosted in Europe and America around the 18th century. Most of these slaves were acquired for peanuts especially when the Europeans induced the African chiefs with their own kind of strong drink called **Rum**.

This practice continued with the blacks going through

most inhumane treatments until their services were no longer needed at the dawn of industrial revolution that swept across Europe in the 19th century. This ushered in the era of colonialism, and an end to slave trade and slavery.

COLONIALISM

In the 19th century, there were new discoveries made in technology that led to an industrial revolution across Europe, before it later spread to America. This means that manual workforce was no longer needed because industries started taking over in production, as machines had substituted human labor.

The output of the industries tremendously surpassed that of the slaves, thus there was high demand for raw materials for industrial production and markets for the goods produced from the industries.

Africa, with its varieties of natural resources, was seen as a viable source of raw materials for industrial production and also as a market for the finished goods. Thus, another scramble to acquire territories in Africa by the European nations such as France, Britain, Portugal and Germany, to control a piece of Africa where they could exploit raw materials for industrial production ensued. This time around, Africans were not bought as slaves but were left in their various communities to raise agricultural and mineral materials which could be bought by the Europeans and taken to Europe for industrial production and the finished goods were brought back for the consumption of Africans. Africa became a dumping ground for European goods. The wealth gotten from African soil was then used to develop the western nations. The agricultural and mineral resources exploited from Nigeria included, cocoa, coal, tin, groundnut, etc. However, some of the repatriated slaves and other Africans back home that acquired Western education began to see reason why Africans should have independent governments of their own. That was when nationalism started and the nationalist leaders who fought for independence later became the founding fathers. The Western powers were not ready to let go of their colonies that they had been exploiting successfully, but because of the pressure mounted by the founding fathers for self-rule, they decided to grant their colonies flag independence. That marked the end of colonial rule in Africa and the start of a new form of colonialism known as neo-colonialism.

NEO-COLONIALISM

In the 20th century, the increased awareness among African elite made them to succeed in acquiring independence for their various nations which were also European creations as a result of the scramble for and partition of Africa when they could just come and capture an area and subject it to be under their home government in Europe. Theoretically, the Africans were said to be granted independence to run their affairs by themselves, but what became the reality being practiced was that most African political leaders became the stooges of the Western powers through which they (Western powers) continued the process of exploiting the mineral resources for their industrial production and still bring back the finished goods for consumption. Nigeria is now an exporter of raw materials and importer of finished goods. It can be conveniently argued that political independence was granted not economic independence. At a point, even toothpick was also imported into Nigeria. Even the Premium Motor Spirit (PMS), a product from crude oil which Nigeria is the sixth largest producer in the world, is still being imported.

This is the new form of colonialism called neo-colonialism. Africa still remains a dumping ground for Western goods. That is where Nigeria has found itself today. Economic policies are tailored towards satisfying the capitalist tendencies of the West with their active Nigerian collaborators. This is achieved through agencies like the International Monetary Fund (IMF), the World Bank, etc. It is one of the reasons why it has become very difficult for Nigeria to build and maintain its refineries to refine petroleum products. Currently, crude oil is still being exploited, taken to the West, refined and brought back for our consumption. There is therefore the dire need for Nigerians to wake up to the realities of foreign domination and control the destiny of the country.

CHAPTER SEVEN

BUILD UP TO 2015

As the country gradually approaches the contentious year two thousand and fifteen (2015) and as the political atmosphere begins to heighten up, the nation is witnessing wrangling from different quarters in the polity as the build up to the general elections of 2015 thickens and continues to gain momentum every day. Each day, the citizens are greeted in the media; both electronic and print, with a fresh event that adds a new twist to the unfolding melodramatic scenario in the largest black nation which also prides itself of having the largest political party in the African continent.

Emerging political scenes are the alignment and realignment that culminate in the merger of some registered political forces; the Action Congress of Nigeria

(ACN), the Congress for Progressive Change (CPC), the All Nigeria People's Party (ANPP) and a faction of the All Progressive Grand Alliance, (APGA). The events leading to the merger of these political parties are believed to have begun shortly after the conduct of the 2011 general elections.

Initially, these talks seemed to be the usual charade that ends up in a deadlock, but subsequent unfolding events were to prove critics of the merger talks wrong because the proponents this time around seemed to have let go their usual personal (selfish interest) considerations and succumbed to collective interest towards forming a formidable opposition that will wrest power from the ruling party (PDP).

Coming up with the idea of registering a political party, the All Progressives Congress (APC) certainly was a master stroke in the camp of the opposition because it caused ripples in some political formations as certain forces felt threatened by this development. The trend of events informed the speculations that the presidency allegedly came up with a political party of the same initials (APC) but different nomenclature, to be registered by the Independent National Electoral Commission (INEC). Another claim to the same nomenclature was made by some other individuals who insisted that INEC had registered them in that name. Even as that controversy was yet to be settled and proposed party awaits INEC registration, the APC masterminded by the ACN, CPC, ANPP, and a faction of APGA, continued to wax stronger and enjoy popular support cutting across all the geo-political zones, political parties, ethnic divides and religious groups. The successful registration of the APC is calculated to upset and unseat the PDP by fielding a Northerner to contest for the presidency in line with the North's pursuit for power to return to the region in 2015.

However, even before the approval by INEC for the new party to come on board, some individuals began to chant some war songs should the current administration lose the election come 2015.

Spearheading this deadly trend is the leader of the Niger Delta Peoples Volunteer Force (NDPVF), Alhaji Mujaheed Asari Dokubo. Asari spoke sequel to a statement made in the United States by the Special Adviser to the President on Niger Delta, Kingsley Kuku that the peace being enjoyed in the Niger Delta will not be guaranteed if President Goodluck Jonathan is not returned in 2015. According to Asari Dokubo, the statement has been supported by several groups in the region. In support of the statement, Asari said *"I want to go on to say that there will be no peace, not only in the Niger Delta, but everywhere if Goodluck Jonathan is not President again, by 2015, except God takes his life, which we don't pray for. Jonathan has uninterrupted eight years of two terms to be president, according to the Nigerian Constitution. We must have our uninterrupted eight years of two tenures; I am not in support of any amendment of the constitution that will reduce the eight years of two tenures that Goodluck Jonathan is expected to be president of Nigeria"*. He said *"for a very long time, our resources from the Niger Delta had been used to feed and fund Nigeria,* and some people are still feeling that Nigeria is their personal property, and they can manage it the way they like, but those days are gone forever; it can never come back." He also said: "A lot of people will say that Goodluck has not performed as President. We from the Niger Delta have been fair. We criticize our own, but that does not change what I have always said that "monkey no fine but him mama like am." The South-south PDP elders and stakeholders forum led by Chief Edwin Clark recently passed a vote of confidence on President Goodluck Jonathan and declared their support for him to contest the presidency come 2015.

In a swift reaction to the statement credited to Alhaji Mujaheed Asari Dokubo, the Northern Youths in a reply said that they were battle ready. The National President of the African Youths, Shuaibu Shinkafi said in an interview he granted journalists that, "the Northern youths are no longer going to tolerate such inciting comments coming from Asari Dokubo and it is totally unacceptable. He is a joker, we have contacted most of *our Youths in all the states in Nigeria to tell them that the lies this government is telling us are unimaginable".*

"We want to tell the whole world that we are not afraid of anybody and if it is violence, we are more violent than Asari Dokubo." He also disclosed that the Northern youths have taken a stand and there will be no going back on it; *"we will not vote for President Goodluck Jonathan come 2015 and therefore in his own interest, he should not even make any attempt to vie for the presidency come 2015, because he is going to meet a strong opposition."*

Some people may decide to wave aside the war of words as mere empty threats, but the tug of war going on in the Governors' Forum is certainly an indication of the shape and nature of the eschatological issues to be expected in 2015. Amidst all these, the Middle Belt which is the stabilizing /unifying factor in the polity, decided to throw its support behind the President, suddenly pulling out of the Northern strategy.

The struggle for 2015 has been extended to the Governor's Forum in their quest to elect a Chairman who will pilot the affairs of the political determinant body. The Rivers State Governor Rotimi Chibuike Amaechi who is widely rumoured to contest the 2015 presidency as a running mate to the Jigawa state Governor, Alhaji Sule Lamido, has been the chairman of the group from 2011 and sought for re-election.

For partnering with a Northern Governor, Amaechi was seen as a betrayer by the South-south with solidarity from the Middle Belt and frantic efforts were made to scuttle his re-election to chair the forum. After the dissolution of the Obio/Akpor Local Government executive by the Rivers State House of Assembly, the PDP National leadership vowed to punish Amaechi. Predictably, it came to pass as an allegedly controversial Abuja High Court judgment of April 15, 2013, removed the state PDP executive led by Chief Godspower Ake, an Amaechi ally, and replaced it with a new executive headed by Chief Felix Obuah backed by the Minister of State for Education Nyesom Wike, known to be pro-Jonathan. The pro-Amaechi executive is in court (Appeal Court) challenging the Abuja High court order. These clearly portray the power play playing out in the quest to control the central Government. Amaechi still went ahead to contest the NGF Chairmanship seat alongside Katsina State's Governor Ibrahim Shema and Isa Yuguda of Bauchi State. The duo was probably the candidates of the President and the PDP. When none of them could give way to the other, a third candidate Jonah Jang of Plateau State emerged as the consensus choice.

In order to ensure victory for its preferred candidate, the PDP mobilized the PDP Governors' Forum to endorse Jang's candidacy. The 19 Northern governors also declared their support for him. But in a twist of events, as the Governors met to ratify their endorsement, a mild drama ensued. Governor Rotimi Amaechi of the oil rich Rivers State was declared winner with 19 votes against Jang with 16 after a secret ballot election that was captured in an eight minutes video. Barely 24 hours later,had some of the disgruntled Governors held a press conference to declare Jang-contrary to the result of the secret ballot voting which they all allegedly subjected themselves to. The Jang group later declared him winner. The incidence has caused a split in the NGF, one that has played into the hands of the opposition and is overheating the Nigerian political scene.

To further reinforce the division in the ruling party, Jang promised to "unite members of the forum and work for the interest of the forum and country." While on the same day Amaechi also made a commitment that "This is the mandate that was freely given and I will stick to that mandate. I think it is up to Nigerians to know that nothing pays more than democracy". Ever since its inception in 1999, the National Governors' Forum has been a PDP stronghold. It has been chaired by five different men, all from the ruling PDP: Abdullahi Adamu of Nasarawa State (1999-2004), Victor Attah, the former Governor of Akwa Ibom State (2004 – 2006), Lucky Igbinedion of Edo State (2006-2011) and most recently Rotimi Amaechi from 2011-2013. As a non-partisan coalition of elected Governors of the 36 states of the federation, the forum *"seeks to promote unity, good governance, better understanding and cooperation among the states and ensure a healthy and beneficial relationship between the states and other tiers of government."*

The NGF's mission statement is, *"To provide a common platform for collaboration amongst the executive governors on matters of public policy; to promote good governance, share of good practice and enhance cooperation at the states and with other arms of government and society."*

Aside these powers of the Nigerian Governors' forum, the body has over the years metamorphosed into a political force to be reckoned with in the nation's politics. Just as Thisdaylive.com captures it thus *"though intended as a voluntary, peer evaluation of association of equals, NGF has grown to become a powerful force in the politics of the country. Largely populated by PDP governors, NGF has been an influential voice in the choice of the ruling party's presidential candidates, and this is hardly surprising. The bulk of the delegates that participate in the voting to choose the presidential candidate are at the governors' beck and call. And the Governors also determine the bulk of those who make it to the Houses of Assembly and the National Assembly. This is in addition to their hold on the Local Government Councils. NGF was instrumental to the abortion of former President Olusegun Obasanjo's widely suspected third term ambition towards the twilight of his second term."* The late President Umaru Yar'adua came from NGF, as Governor of Katsina State, to win nomination as PDP Presidential candidate in 2007. And the incumbent President, Jonathan, was Governor of Bayelsa State when he was nominated as running mate to Yar'adua." Both men were presented to the NGF by former President Olusegun Obasanjo. By these developments, Jonathan is aware of the influence of the Governors to his yet-to-be announced second term ambition. Therefore, it is political sense for both camps to strive to be in control of the forum. This is the politics being played at the NGF and subsequent election.

However, to further widen the gap in the political circles

and the build up to 2015, the likes of former President Olusegun Obasanjo, General Ibrahim Babangida and Alhaji Atiku Abubakar have been assumed to be in opposition to Goodluck Jonathan's second term ambition. In a statement made by former President Olusegun Obasanjo at the first Jigawa State Investment Forum on 1st May 2013, hosted by the man perceived to be his preferred candidate, Alhaji Sule Lamido, Obasanjo observed that "you can help someone to get a job but you cannot help that person to do the job." This was seen as a thinly veiled broadside against the incumbent president. As part of the multifaceted battle for the soul of the most populous country in Africa, there are many controversies within the ruling party; the Northern Governors' Forum is no longer united as allegiances have been divided. The proposed constitution review that sought to amend the constitution in respect of the tenure of political office holders from four years of one term that can be renewed to a single term of six (6) years did not receive favorable support from the National Assembly either. The proposed amendment, if passed into law, is to take effect from

2015.

In the opening chapter of this book which was written about a year before these antecedents, it was stated that come 2015, the Northerners were going to lay claim to the presidency and that they would put up a good fight for it, especially now that the PDP zoning formula principle has been put to rest. Thus, the political landscape continues to heat up as the political forces strategize on how to wrest power come 2015. The threats are becoming more glaring, making it pertinent to note that adhering to the calls by progressive proponents for a true federalist state is the way out. Events leading to the 2015 general elections took another swift dimension when the Independent National Electoral Commission (INEC) observed that some of the members of the National Executive Committee of the People's Democratic Party, PDP, were not duly elected into various positions of the party's leadership in contrast to laid down rules and so these officials were not officially recognized by INEC. In its bid not to allow abnormality to throw a spanner in the wheel of their progress towards the 2015 general elections, the ruling PDP promptly declared the affected positions vacant and went ahead to organize a mini-National Convention to replace the affected officers.

Prior to this, intra-party wrangling in the PDP was posing greater challenges towards the party's smooth conduct of its mini convention when a splinter group the "G7 governors" emerged as a result of the fallout of the election of the Nigerian Governors' forum. The G7 demanded for the replacement of some of the officers whose offices were affected by INEC's proclamation especially the office of the National Secretary.

While this went on, an application for registration by five political parties to merge as one political party by the four political parties that came under the umbrella of the All Progressives Congress was granted by INEC, presenting a viable opposition to the ruling and dangling PDP. In quick succession, other political parties were registered which included the Independent Democrats (IG), the People's Democratic Movement (PDM) etc., as each group increasingly sought relevance and for alternative platforms for some people in other political parties to fall back to in the event that the need arises.

However, at the special mini convention of the PDP, having the feelers that their interest was not going to be protected, the G7 Governors, together with the former Vice-president of the Federal Republic of Nigeria, Alhaji Atiku Abubakar and their supporters decided to stage a walkout at the Eagle Square, venue of the convention, including all their delegates, and converged on the Shehu Musa Yar'adua Conference Center where others were said to have been waiting for their arrival.

In a speech by Baraje whom the group recognized as its own chairman, they expressed their grievances with the BamangaTukur led faction of the PDP and declared itself the original PDP. He (Baraje) listed some of the "sins" of the BamangaTukur faction to include the highhanded treatment of some members of the party especially the suspension of the Sokoto State Governor, Alhaji Aliyu Wammako, who was later recalled; the suspension of Governor Chibuike Ameachi of Rivers State; the sacking of the Rivers State executive and replacing them with an executive that is seen by them as pro-Jonathan; and also the refusal of the Bamanga Tukur led faction to go along with their initial agreement that those officers whose offices were affected, be returned at the convention.

Baraje made a declaration that based on the above and other salient issues, the original founding members of the party decided to take that bold step to salvage the party from those who did not know how the party was formed in the first place, therefore claiming their faction to be the authentic PDP. He listed the conditions consequent to their return back into the main stream to include; the reversal of the suspension placed on Governor Rotimi Ameachi of Rivers state, and the restoration of the suspended Rivers State executive, the immediate removal of Tukur as Chairman, recognition of Amaechi as Chairman of the Nigerian Governors Forum, and finally that a fresh convention of the party be held.

These prompted series of meetings between the Governors of the new PDP and the Presidency to come to terms in finding a lasting solution to the impasse within the party. The demand of the G7 Governors is considered not feasible by the Presidency, thus increasing the level of animosity in the already tensed political atmosphere within the party and in the nation as a whole.

In order to emphasize on the seriousness of their demands, the G7 Governors later visited the National Assembly at the resumption of plenary to table their grievances before the leadership of the Senate and the House of Representatives. This development led to a clash between House of Representative members supporting the main PDP and those supporting the new PDP in the green hallowed chambers of the National Assembly in the full glare of press men's inquisitive cameras that captured all the show of shame for the consumption of the general public.

Reacting to the turn of events, the Senate President, David Mark, observed with dismay the turn of events and lamented how the country was gradually dwindling into a failed state; he thus suggested that it was high time a National Conference was convened so as to discuss issues of urgent national importance. This observation received wide range of commendations from Nigerians from all walks of life that saw it as a welcome development. Even as Nigerians cutting across the six geo-political zones applauded this suggestion, some like the Afenifere are still not satisfied with a National Conference (NC), but rather are canvassed for a Sovereign National Conference (S.N.C).

Sequel to the suggestion by the Senate President and the applause it received from Nigerians, the President of the Federal Republic of Nigeria, Dr. Goodluck Jonathan decided that there shall be a National Conference, considering the logjam in the polity and the popular calls for convening of such, thus in his independence speech on 1st October 2013, he listed the names of members of an advisory committee for the national confab. The membership of the committee comprises of:-

1. Senator Femi Akorounmu –Chairman

2. Prof. George Obiozo

4. Prof. Ben Nwabweze

5. Khairat Gwadabe

6. Timothy Adudu

7. Col. Tony Nyiam (rtd)

8. Prof. Funke Adebayo

9. Abubakar Ahmed Amshi

10. Dauda Birma

11. Buhari Bello

12. Tony Uranta

13. Akilu Ndabawa –Secretary

The task assigned to the committee was to consult with stakeholders and draw up an agenda for the proposed national conference. It is expected to make recommendations to the FG on the structure, modalities and time frame for the proposed National Conference and to make recommendations to the Government on the determination of the various interest groups to be presented at the conference. In justifying the step taken, the president stated that " when there are issues that constantly stoke tension and bring about friction, it makes perfect sense for the interested parties to come together to discuss."

HEIGHTENING STATE OF INSECURITY

Meanwhile, as political manipulations increase in tempo, the level of security of lives and property of citizens has been on the decrease. The activities of the Boko Haram sect got worsened with attacks on military and para-military forces killing them in their numbers. The sect unleashed terror on the towns of Baga and Bama where so many soldiers and mobile police men lost their lives. The height of siege by the Boko Haram was when the Nigerian national flag was brought down in some parts of Borno and Yobe states, replacing them with some foreign colors. Though a state of emergency has been declared on the states of Yobe, Borno and Adamawa, pundits are of the opinion that a more lasting solution should be an unraveling of the political under-tone to the impasse.

Another security threat is the massacre of mobile police men and men of the State Security Service (SSS) who were on a mission to arrest the head of a cult group (OMBATSE) in Nassarawa State, who were allegedly terrorizing the area. Government sources gave the total figure of security agents killed to be forty-six (46) while the head of the cult claimed that almost a hundred security agents were massacred. This deadly trend can only suggest the kind of power play and the desperate quest for power.

While these events were happening in Nasarawa State, the South-East and South-South parts of the country were turned into arenas of kidnapping. This has become a means of making quick money for the perpetrators ever since armed robbery became non-profitable to them because people no longer keep money at home. Thus, the kidnap of a loved one will force relatives to pay a ransom to have such a person back. Therefore, in a country where security operatives are slaughtered like animals and 'everything is left in the hands of God,' as the head of the state security service declared, who else is safe. What can the ordinary citizens do? Should they leave everything in the hands of God to come down and determine their fate? No, people should rather commit themselves to God and take their future in their hands while insisting that the appropriate thing be done, at this juncture – true federalism is the way out.

Furthermore, the activities of the Fulani cattle rearers who traverse not only the length and breadth of Nigeria but that of the entire African continent, add another dangerous dimension to the issue of insecurity in the country. These people go about looking for grazing land for their cattle. In Nigeria, most of the routes taken by the herdsmen are populated by local farmers, whose crops are usually tempered with by the cattles and their only source of drinking water; the rivers, usually are contaminated by these cattle. This results into deadly clashes between the farmers and the Fulani men. These have been the cause of killing of many innocent lives especially women and children by these herdsmen who value their cows more than human lives. This case was particularly persistent on the Jos Plateau where hundreds of lives including that of a serving Senator and a member of the State House of Assembly, were lost to the barbaric attacks. It later spread to other parts of the country like Benue, Anambra and Oyo States. A true federalist state will surely provide a permanent grazing land for the herdsmen that will be devoid of unnecessary confrontation.

CONCLUSION

The inability of both military and civilian administrations to address Nigeria's intractable challenges of ethnicity, religious bigotry, corruption, economic deprivation and insecurity sincerely led to the following challenges which are presently threatening the very existence of the country. These include; Political tension resulting from ethnic nationalism, conflicting cleavages, corrupt system that is self-serving and opportunistic in an effort to control the Government at the centre.

Alleged widespread corruption at all levels of governance, self-serving political gambits, alarming dimension of looting and theft of Government financial resources by various political office holders in Government with little or no sanctions, robbery, kidnapping, hired killers, political assassinations, sectional killings and other indecent, often violent militant activities.

Boko Haram insurgency is the most incredible vicious and poverty driven/politically induced destructive terrorism ravaging most parts of the Northern states of Nigeria and the Federal Capital Territory, Abuja, causing sorrow among the generality of Nigerians.

Pervasive poverty and unemployment in the population exacerbated by non-existent economic industrial base and/or a competitive industrial economy; contaminated educational value, low standards in academic and institutions that have become centers for certificate acquisition through fraught with examination collapse leading to a situation in which Nigerian Universities which used to rank within the first ten (10) in the world before 1970 now struggle to be mentioned within the first 1500;

Science and technology activities are in near total exclusion of domestic indigenous capability and/or capacity building for Research and Development (R&D), engineering design and fabrication, technology production and technology innovation leaving the sustenance of the economy to the vagaries of foreign produced technologies, industrial goods and foreign professionals; Pronounced inadequacy in critical economic development supporting infrastructure including electrical power supply (the prime energy for sustaining competitive manufacturing sector of the economy), wealth creation and employment generation in the economy; An over bloated national political federal administration in which well over 75% of budget is being spent on servicing the bureaucracy leaving less than 25% for capital projects in support of critical socio-economic development activities.

All the challenges mentioned above are consequences of the abandonment of true federalism and the concentration of power in the centre. In the next section, a return to true federalism to save Nigeria from impending calamity shall be advocated.

PART TWO

THE WAY OUT

Despite the myriad of challenges that constitute threats to the nation in its determination to remain one indivisible and virile entity in peace unity and progress, there is a way out. The ways out of Nigeria's logjam which shall be enumerated in this part include true federalism, visionary and incorruptible leadership and the Nigerian spirit (patriotism).

CHAPTER EIGHT

TRUE FEDERALISM

The only peaceful way out of the myriad of threats posed to the corporate existence of Nigeria as an entity is a return to the practice of true federalism to capture fairly all interests of Nigerian ethnic nationalities. To have an appraisal of the concept of true federalism, there is the need to understand what federalism is all about, how and why it was adopted in Nigeria, how it thrived and why it was thwarted and jettisoned.

THE IDEA OF FEDERALISM

The concept of federalism has been defined in various ways by different scholars, based on how they perceived the term. There is a classical version and there are other versions. In the process of defining the concept, many scholars have been willingly saddled with descriptive normative and prescriptive commitment, depending on their individual interest and intellectual perspective. While some scholars define federalism from the perspective of the description of political arrangement in an existing system, others define it from the perspective of what ought to be or what should be based on their analysis of the geo-political arrangement in existence or potential political systems.

Most of the contemporary writers on federalism have their intellectual origin in the work of Kenneth C. Wheare, despite observed differences in emphasis. In his epochal thesis on federalism, Kenneth C. Wheare said that it entails;

A division of powers between one general and several regional governments, each of which in its own sphere is coordinate with the others; each government must act directly on the people, each must be united to its sphere of action, and each must within that sphere be independent of the others.

The critical ingredients that can be deduced from Kenneth Wheare's definition of federalism are that for any political system to be so described, it must have;

(a)   Two or more locus of power where values can

(b)   be authoritatively allocated.

(c)   A central government and co-ordination level (tiers) of government each of   which must be recognized as a functional unit by the constitution.

(d)   Constitutionally recognized areas of competence and process of interaction. Wheare also identifies six important conditions precedent to the existence of federal arrangement, which are:

A.   Previous experience of the federating states as distinct colonies or states with distinct   governments of their own.

B.   A divergence of economic interest between the federating states leading to the   desire of the state to remain economically independent for certain economic

     purposes.

C.   Geographical   obstacles   to   effective   unitary government that is a large area and   poor communication which includes;

i.   Differences   of   race,   religion,   language   of nationality.

ii.   Dissimilarity of social institutions

ii.   Force of imitation that is, the prior existence of a

federal constitution to serve as a   model.

In his own definition, Birch suggested that: "*A federal system of government is one on which there is a division of powers between one general and several regional authorities each of which in its own sphere is co-ordinate with the others and each of which acts directly on the people through its own administrative agencies.*"

Federalism is a dual form of government based on a territorial and functional division of powers calculated to reconcile unity with diversity. In a similar view, Long has defined federalism as an institutional arrangement aimed at addressing governmental problems that border on maintaining unity while at the same time preserving diversity. It has been offered as an institutional solution in the disruptive tendencies of inter-societal ethnic pluralism. Another suggestion is that federalism is but a device for the management of diversity. These definitions presuppose the existence of opposing and often conflicting groups and interests in the state, all of which must have to be accommodated in an overarching national union through pulling them apart. Akande defines federalism as a process of bringing equilibrium between the centrifugal and centripetal forces in the society.

It has also been defined as a methodology of limited union directed to the production of limited unity. This is because it allows units to exercise jurisdictional control over their territories which also provide hegemony for national institutions. It makes this possible through a constitutional power sharing arrangement between the central and units of government in such a manner that the jurisdiction of each level is recognized and constitutionally protected. Such an arrangement has the advantage of managing or reducing conflict that may arise from inter relationship between the diverse groups or units in the state.

In the light of all the above definitions, it can be concluded that federalism represents an institutional mechanism through which intra-societal plural elements can be accommodated and protected.

This conclusion can be applied to the Nigerian situation. Nigeria became a federalist state at independence as a result of provisions in the Richards Constitution of 1951 and the Littleton Constitution of 1954 which laid the foundation for takeoff. Therefore, a lot of factors necessitated the choice of federalism as a form of government for the Nigerian state, which the British colonialists and the Nigerian founding fathers found to be adequately appropriate for a viable Nigeria and to continue to foster unity in diversity.

FACTORS THAT NECESSITATED THE PRACTICE OF FEDERALISM IN NIGERIA

Prior to British colonization of Nigeria as earlier noted, there was no geographical entity called Nigeria. The component units of the federation were separate entities that had little or nothing in common, but these component units were amalgamated to become one entity by Lord Lugard in 1914. Hence, these realities of our historical past made federalism to be attractive to the nationalist leaders before independence.

Another reason why the nationalist leaders and the British colonialist considered federalism as a form of government was the population and land mass, most especially after the amalgamation of 1914. Nigeria's land mass is 913,070304 square miles, while the population of Nigeria today is estimated to be between 170 and 180 million.

Religious difference which today has sparked off a lot of crisis most especially in the Northern part of the country was one of the reasons why federalism was considered as a viable option for Nigeria. Nigeria has three major religious groups; Christianity, Islam and traditional religious belief. Traditional religious belief does not always promote bigotry as the other two.

Ethnicity was another reason for opting for the practice of federalism in the first republic in Nigeria. Nigeria has over 300 ethnic groups; Hausa Fulani in the North, the Yoruba in the west and the Igbo in the East. The minority groups together are more or less equal to the big three combined together. Economic diversification is another reason for the adoption of federalism as a system of government. As the country is vast in land mass and numerous in ethnic groups so also the way and manner in which the various economic activities of the people differ. This is more so because of the geographical differences across the length and breadth of the country.

Social and cultural institutions formed by the multiple ethnic nationalities and the imposing nature of the British federal system were also among the considerations for the practice of federalism in Nigeria.

The British are the most federal of all races, they created a large number of federations in different parts of the world and the Nigerian case was in tandem with the British instinct whose crave for federalism had become a bye word in the twentieth century. The practice was also a strategy for decolonization, which is either proposed by the British colonial authorities to reduce cost of colonial administration as in east and central Africa or to stem internal division tendencies as obtained in Nigeria. However, the biggest challenge which subsequently prompted the choice of federalism was the uncompromising attitude of Nigerian nationalist leaders, which led to the fractionalization of politics.

The National Council of Nigeria and Cameroon (NCNC) ceased to enjoy nation-wide support because of its tribal political coloration which was, in fact, an offshoot of cultural organizations developed in 1949, in the North and in 1950, in the West. The Northern People Congress (NPC) and Action Group (AG) from this time began to play dominant roles in constitution making.

The Action Group (AG) led by Chief Obafemi Awolowo developed from the Egbe Omo Oduduwa founded in 1948, and the NPC led by Sir Ahmadu Bello developed from the Jam'iyar Mutanen Arewa, which was founded in Kano in December, 1949 by the educated elite in the North, particularly Aminu Kano and AbubakarTafawa Balewa among others. With the emergence of these regional parties, the question of what type of federalism Nigeria was to have become the subject of negotiation between the parties. Nigeria's unity was still not on secure ground and whenever a party felt sufficiently aggrieved over issues, the natural thing for it to do was to threaten to secede from the federation. Indeed, for convergence of reasons, none of the regional leaders was ready to surrender or sacrifice his region for a unitary state that would brew suspicion and fear of domination or hegemony. Hence, federalism became attractive to them all. After the amalgamation of the Northern and Southern protectorates in 1914, the British administration introduced the practice of unitary government in Nigeria through the provinces. This was done by subdividing the protectorates into provinces like in the cases of Adamawa, Bornu, Kano provinces of the Northern protectorates, Abeokuta, Ondo, Delta, etc., of the western protectorates and Onitsha, Owerri, etc., provinces of the Eastern protectorates respectively. The provincial Administrators were to report through their respective Lt Governors to the Governor General in Lagos which was the capital of the unitary based colonial administration. This administrative arrangement was unacceptable to Nigerian ethnic nationalities. Therefore, to keep the constituent ethnic nationalities as one nation, the British had to opt for a new constitutional arrangement in 1950 and federalism was seen as the beautiful bride.

In a unanimous rejection of the unitary form of government, the leaders of the respective ethnic nationalities took the following position at a conference at

Ibadan in 1951: Alhaji Sir Ahmadu Bello of the British Northern Nigeria stated that "the North is for the Northern people, West for the people of the West and East for the people of the East and Lagos the capital for us all." Chief Obafemi Awolowo of the British Western Nigeria stated that "North is for the North, West for the West, East for the east but Lagos as part of the west belongs to the west" and Dr. Nnamdi Azikwe of the ethnic nationalities of the British Eastern Nigeria agreed with both Alhaji Sir Ahmadu Bello and Chief Obafemi Awolowo but had to differ on the position of Lagos, which he suggested should be independent of all the three regions and to serve as an independent capital of the evolving federal union state of Nigeria. Similarly the British over Lords could not have pretended not to know that it was the most appropriate for a heterogeneous society like Nigeria, though other personal considerations may follow. Added to this is that the British would not have imposed federalism in the country if circumstances had dictated otherwise. In other words, adoption of federalism in Nigeria was neither an exclusive action of the British nor that of the nationalist leaders alone but rather it was a mutual desire of the two parties.

However, the British convened a conference of Nigeria's ethnic nationalities at Ibadan in western Nigeria in 1954 to discuss and agree on the terms of union. The conference was reported to have decided unanimously to set up a federal structure administration under a well worked out and agreed terms of union as the best option to sustaining peace, in Nigeria as a nation. The only certain fact that became obvious about the origin and rationale for federalism in Nigeria was that certain objective factors made federalism desirable if the country was to remain united. Hence, one can hardly query the foresight of the nationalist leaders who, out of the desire for self rule opted for the federal solution.

HOW NIGERIA FARED UNDER TRUE FEDERALISM AND THE FACTORS THAT MADE IT POSSIBLE

The prevailing circumstances, the geographical and human barriers and the position taken by the founding fathers eventually led to the acceptance of federalism in 1954 as a form of administration to govern the nation. This position was reached at a conference in Ibadan in 1954, when the British colonial authority and the ethnic national leaders agreed on the terms of union for a federation of Nigerian nationalities comprising Northern Nigeria nationalities, Western Nigeria nationalities, and Eastern Nigeria nationalities respectively. Lagos was the capital of the federal government and Kaduna, Ibadan and Enugu respectively were the capitals of Northern, Western and Eastern regional governments respectively.

The specific terms agreed upon for the union are namely that each regional government should:

(1)   Take full control and responsibility for and develop its resources (human and natural primary raw materials) and other endowments.

(2)   Control exclusively the education of its citizens at the primary and secondary   level   but   share responsibility with the federal government in establishing Universities in order to allow the existing University College, Ibadan, established   by   the   colonial

administration to continue to be for all the regions and to be administered by the federal government, but that all the secondary schools established by the British colonial administration in each respective region should be taken over by the respective regional governments.

(3)   Contribute 50% of its export revenue derived from its region to a distributive pool for all Nigerians and keep 50% exclusively to itself. However, the federal government, which had no land resources for economic activities but a capital territory, should contribute nothing and should keep for itself the personal income tax derived from all Nigerian citizens working for the federal government.

(4)   Out of contributions from federating regional government to national financial   pool, the budget requirement for the running of Federal Government should   be worked out and passed on to the Federal Government. The balance of the contributions should be divided equally into four parts one each to each of the three federating regional governments and one to the Federal Government itself.

(5)   The responsibilities of the federal government specifically are common services, namely defense, the military, police, immigration, customs, Central Bank, foreign affairs including foreign trade and investments, railings telecommunications,   national   industrial products standards but any residual responsibility   not specifically mentioned for the federal government should be the responsibility of the federating regional governments.

However, land, agriculture and other economic activities remained exclusively the responsibility of the federating regions. Because of the terms of union agreed upon by all parties concerned, which is now referred to as true federalism, the regional governments of Nigeria began to operate competitively among themselves in equity, peace, harmony and progress. During the revenue distribution exercise of 1954, the Western region of

Nigeria had the highest revenue of £45 million pound sterling from the distribution pool, Northern Nigeria £35 million pound sterling, Federal Government £30 million pounds sterling and Eastern Nigeria, £10 million pound sterling which was the lowest allocation. Therefore, according to Felix Oragwu the Igbo ethnic nationality led Eastern Nigeria, known at least before 1970 for its core culture and belief in hard work, effort, innovation, adventure, integrity, maximum self-reliance and the "brother's keeper mantra" was able with the lowest £10 million pound sterling's revenue allocation of 1954, to leapfrog into the fastest growing economy in West Africa by 1964. A healthy competition was being engendered to the extent that each region had to muster its human resources to exploit the natural resources and maximize same for economic growth. That was the state of affairs before the military incursion into governance in 1966.

HOW, WHEN AND WHY NIGERIA DEVIATED FROM THE PRACTICE OF TRUE FEDERALISM

The equity, peace, harmony and progress that were enjoyed by the federating units and the federal government of Nigeria from 1954 were hampered and disrupted when the military decided to strike and take over power from the civilian administration on January 15th 1966.

A series of antecedents preceded the decision of the military to take over power from the civilians, but the most crucial factor was the political logjam that the country found itself in. Due to the split into the three geo-political regions, party politics (and political parties) took on the identity and ideology of each of the three regions.

The Northern region was represented by the Northern People's Congress (NPC) dominated by the Hausa-Fulani while the Western regions' dominant party was the Yoruba Action Group (AG) and East's National Council of Nigeria Citizens (NCNC) which was controlled by the Igbo.

The NPC took control of the Federal Government with the NCNC as the junior partner in a shaky coalition (the NPC's deputy head, Tafawa Balewa became the Prime Minister and then Nnamdi Azikiwe took the ceremonial role of President). The AG led the opposition. The make-up of the government was odd because the NPC leader, Sir Ahmadu Bello, could have become the Prime Minister but chose to instead become the head of Northern Region, and handed over the Prime Minister's chair to his deputy Tafawa Balewa. Rightly or wrongly, many southern politicians viewed Balewa as Bello's puppet and resented the fact that (in their opinion) the government was being ruled by proxy by a regional ruler and viewed Bello as the real power beyond the throne. This may have led southern politicians to have a disrespectful attitude towards Balewa. This perception was not helped when Bello referred to Balewa as "my lieutenant in Lagos." At independence, the Northern region was given more seats in parliament than the two southern regions put together. This meant that no meaningful governmental decision affecting Nigeria could be taken without the consent of the North. Southern rulers belatedly began to appreciate the fact that Northern politicians were not as naïve as they thought and the lopsided parliament meant that the North would politically control Nigeria forever. The only way to alter the Northern control of the country was through a constitutional amendment (unlikely since the North controlled the parliament)...... or violence. The conviction and imprisonment of the AG leaders and the western region's premier, Chief Obafemi Awolowo, for treason created the impression that some southerners had chosen the latter option. In a controversial trial, Awolowo was convicted of hatching a plot to overthrow the government by force of arms. Awolowo's incarceration was followed by the installation of an unpopular government led by Chief Samuel Akintola of the NNDP. The NNDP has very close links with the ruling NPC and was regarded by many as a subsidiary of the NPC. Akintola was elected premier of the western region in a bitterly controversial election that was widely regarded as massively rigged. Popular resentment against NNDP spilled over to wide scale violence, protests, arsons and murders that placed many parts of the western region into a state of near anarchy which earned the region the nickname of the "wild west".

The NPC government decided to authorize a massive security crackdown to curb the lawlessness in the west. Additionally, the corruption of certain government ministers drew public condemnation. The ostentatious lifestyle of government ministers such as Chief Festus

Okotie-Eboh raised eyebrows to say the least. It became clear that a violent conflict was inevitable in view of mumblings of possible military coup as early as 1964. President Azikiwe (in his position of Commander in Chief of the country's armed forces) had openly called on the army to intervene to break the political deadlock in the country after he refused to call Balewa to form a new government following scandalous elections that were marred by massive rigging, thuggery, intimidation and murder.

The heads of the Army, Navy and Air force all met with Azikiwe and made it clear that they would not intervene. Azikiwe also obtained legal advice from the Attorney General which indicated that the service chiefs were right to disobey his call to intervene. Azikiwe, therefore, eventually called on Balewa to form a new government after the nation tottered perilously in the murky waters of uncertainty.

Hence, out of the fear of certain anticipated political decisions which might have involved the use of the army to forcefully restore order in the Akintola-led western region and cram the results of the controversial October 1965 election down the throat of voters, the coup was finally launched on January 15th 1966 by some junior officers in the military. The coup failed to bring the young "Turks" who led it to power but it did result to a complex and controversial series of events in the emergence of a military regime led by General Ironsi.

However, it is evident that the coup and the subsequent military take over seemed to be a little hasty because a political solution to the controversial issues which had started by dialogue was in the offing. The paradox of this alleged NPC plan to wallop the west was that the late Prime Minister, Tafawa Balewa, in his last interview just before the coup, was actually contemplating a political solution to the impasse in the western region; one that might have involved a coalition government and the release of Chief Obafemi Awolowo. The last interview granted to the magazine "*West Africa*" by the late Prime Minister Balewa on January 14th, 1966 some few hours to his death went thus:

Question: *Do you see the solution as taking the form of a* *coalition government in the west?*

Balewa: Yes, it would have to be that... the Action Group has accepted my mediation but the NNDP has asked for time. If I use real force in the west, and make no mistake about it, I haven't yet,and then I could bring the people to their knees. But I did not want to use force like that. Force can't bring peace to people's hearts.

Question: Would you consider the release of Chief Awolowo as part of a political solution of the west's trouble?

Balewa:I think that might be part of it; yes, obviously we would have to see.

From the above, it can be observed that dialogue would have been the best option to unravel the deadlock that occurred in the political arena. The same dialogue necessitated the choice of the option of federalism earlier by the founding fathers and the British authorities.

However, the military under the command of General Aguiyi Ironsi who became Head of State decided to suspend all provisions of the constitution and replaced it with decrees. Consequently, Decree 34 of 1966 was attempted to translate Nigeria from being a federal system to a unitary system. That attempt cost Aguiyi Ironsi his life and that of his administration. But subsequent military administrations tried to maintain the Federalist system but in real practice, it was a centralized command, as is the tradition in the military.

Inspite of its inherent and perceivable imperfections, Nigeria was still perceived as a federal entity until the military seized the reins of government in January 1966. The military, by training and orientation, is an institution attuned to centralized command.

Its hierarchical structure creates a situation where order flows from the top. In seizing political power, the military maintained its tradition of centrality of authority but also attempted to regiment the civilian population. It carried it to absurdity when General Ironsi attempted to turn Nigeria into a unitary state by Decree 34 of 1966. The attempt not only led to the collapse of his administration and his death and set in motion the phenomenon of counter coups as revenge mechanism.

Successive military rulers (regimes) continued in that

fashion and even the civil administrations of Alhaji Shehu Shagari, 1979 -1983, General Olusegun Obasanjo (rtd) 1999 – 2007, Alhaji Musa Umar Yar'adua (late), 2007-2010 and the current President, Goodluck Jonathan 2010 till date, continued with the culture of centralized command where the centre has abrogated more powers to itself at the detriment of state and local government areas. It is expected that with the return to civil rule, the process of dialogue as initiated by the founding fathers and the British authorities, should be continued in finding a lasting solution to the diverse problems.

Since the return to civil rule, many people from different quarters have lent their voices to the agitation for a return to the practice of true federalism. However, there are fears in some quarters, especially in the North, that resource control will leave them impoverished because of the perception that crude oil is the only dollar spinning resource in Nigeria. But facts have shown that every state of the federation is adequately endowed with vast mineral resources to sustain itself economically. The economic realities that support this fact shall be discussed below.

QUEST FOR TRUE FEDERALISM AND ECONOMIC REALITIES

Nigeria is richly endowed with mineral resources, tourism potentials and agricultural products that can support a viable true federal structure. There is no state or region in Nigeria that is not adequately blessed. For the continued existence of the country as an entity, government needs to retrace its steps and begin to execute true justice in the land which includes aggressive development of moribund agrarian and tourism potentials together with optimal mining and management of mineral resources. Mineral exploitation and management of solid mineral resources alongside the neglect of other economic sectors can boost the country's economy.

In the agricultural sector, it has been discovered in 1990 that eighty-two (82) million hectares are found to be arable, although only 42% of the cultivable land area was cultivated. Much of this land was farmed under the bush fallow system whereby land is left idle for a period of time to allow natural regeneration of soil fertility. Eighteen (18) million hectares were classified as permanent pasture, but had the potential to support crops. Most of the twenty (20) million hectares covered by forest and wood land are believed to have agricultural potentials. Agriculture contributes 32% of GDP and mostly simple tools are used. This arable land is found in all the states of the federation and even in the desert areas of the North while the soil type supports the growth of certain types of crops and even in commercial quantities.

In the tourism sector, it is a known fact that it has become a global sustainable revenue earner, competing favorably with the manufacturing sector, especially in the developed countries. However, in spite of the enormous tourism potentials in Nigeria, the industry's contribution to the economic development in the country is not encouraging. The 2011 report by World Travel and Tourism Council (WTTC) shows that the direct contribution of travel and tourism to Nigeria's GDP in 2011 was N598.6 billion (1.6% of GDP). As positive as this result is, tourism market in Nigeria still has a long way to go. The WTTC forecasts that this figure has the capacity rise by 11% to N664.6 billion in 2012. This primarily reflects the economic activities generated by industries such as hotels, travel agents, air lines, other passenger transportation service, restaurants and leisure industries directly supported by tourists. This is an indication of the enormous potential that lies within the under developed tourism industry in Nigeria. Resource control, an ingredient of true federalism, will afford the states the opportunity to look inwards, develop and market their tourism potential for wealth generation.

In the mining sector, it is an overwhelming fact that every state of the federation including the Federal Capital Territory is immensely endowed with mineral resources in commercial quantities which can generate billions of dollars to the respective states where they are found. The mining of minerals in Nigeria accounts for only 0.3% of its GDP due to the influence of its vast oil resources.

Below is a table showing the distribution of mineral resources available in each state of Nigeria.

Nigerian States and Their Natural Resources: TABLE 1

S/N	STATES	NATURAL RESOURCES
1	Abia	Gold, Lead/Zinc, Limestone, Oil/Gas & Salt
2	Abuja	Cassiterite, Clay, Dolomite, Gold, Lead/Zinc, Marble & Tantalite
3	Adamawa	Bentonite, Gypsium, Kaolin & Magnesite
4	Akwa Ibom	Clay, Lead/Zinc, Lignite, Limestone, Oil/Gas, Salt & Uranium
5	Anambra	Clay, Glass-Sand, Gypsium, Iron-ore, Lead/Zinc, Lignite, Limestone, Phosphate & Salt
6	Bauchi	Gold, Cassiterite (tine ore), Columbite, Gypsium, Wolfram, Coal, Limestone, Lignite, Iron-ore & Clay
7	Bayelsa	Glay, Gypsium, Lead/Zinc, Lignite, Limestone, Maganese, Oil/Gas & Uranium
8	Benue	Barite, Clay, Coal, Gemstone, Gypsium, Iron-Ore, Lead/Zinc, Limestone, Marble & Salt
9	Borno	Bentonite, Clay, Diatomite, Gypsium,

		Hydro-carbon, Kaolin & Limestone
10	Cross River	Barite, Lead/Zinc, Lignite, Limestone, Manganese, Oil/Gas, Salt & Uranium
11	Delta	Clay, Glass-sand, Gypsium, Iron-ore, Kaolin, Lignite, Marble & Oil/Gas
12	Ebonyi	Gold, Lead/Zinc & Salt
13	Edo	Bitumen, Clay Dolomite, Phosphate, Glass-sand, Gold, Gypsium,Iron-ore, Lignite, Limestone, Marble & Oil/Gas
14	Ekiti	Feldspar, Granite, Kaolin, Syenite & Tatium
15	Enugu	Coal, Lead/Zinc & Limestone
16	Gombe	Gemstone & Gypsium
17	Imo	Gypsium, Lead/Zinc, Lignite, Limestone, Marcasite, Oil/Gas, Phosphate & Salt
18	Jigawa	Butyles
19	Kaduna	Amethyst, Aqua Marine, Asbestos, Clay, Flosper,

		Gemstone, Gold, Graphite, Kaolin, Hyanite, Mica, Rock
		Crystal, Ruby, Sapphire, Sihnite, Superntinite, Tentalime,
		Topaz & Tourmaline
20	Kano	Gassiterite, Copper, Gemstone, Glass-sand, Lead/Zinc, Pyrochinre & Tantalite
21	Katsina	Kaolin, Marble & Salt
22	Kebbi	Gold
23	Kogi	Cole, Dolomite, Feldspar, Gypsium, Iron-ore, Kaolin, Marble, Talc & Tantalite
24	Kwara	Cassiterite, Columbite, Feldspar, Gold, Iron-ore, Marble, Mica & Tantalite
25	Lagos	Bitumen, Clay & Glass-sand
26	Nasarawa	Amethyst (Topaz Garnet), Barytex, Barite, Cassirite, Chalcopyrite, Clay, Columbite, Coking Coal, Dolomite/Marble, Feldspar, Galena,

		Iron-ore, Limstone, Mica, Salt, Sapphire, Talc, Tantalite, Tourmaline Quartz & Zireon
27	Niger	Gold, Lead/Zinc & Talc
28	Ogun	Bitumen, Clay, Feldspar, Gemstone, Kaolin, Limestone & Phosphate
29	Ondo	Bitumen, Clay, Coal, Dimension Stones, Feldspar, Gemstone, Glass-Sand, Granite, Gypsium, Kaolin, Limestone & Oil/Gas
30	Osun	Columbite, Gold, Granite, Talc, Tantalite & Tourmaline
31	Oyo	Aqua Marine, Cassiterite, Clay, Dolomite, Gemstone, Gold, Kaolin, Marble, Silimonite, Talc & Tantalite
32	Plateau	Barite, Bauxite, Betonite, Bismuth, Cassiterite, Clay, Coal, Emeral, Fluoride, Gemstone, Granite, Iron-ore,

		Kaolin, Lead/Zinc, Marble, Molybdenite, Phrochlore, Salt, Tantalite/Columbite, Tin & Wolfram
33	Rivers	Clay, Glass-Sand, Lignite, Marble & Oil/Gas
34	Sokoto	Clay, Flakes, Gold, Granite, Gypsium, Kaolin, Laterite, Limestone, Phosphate, Potash, Silica Sand & Salt
35	Taraba	Lead/Zinc
36	Yobe	Soda Ash & Tintomite
37	Zamfara	Coal, Cotton & Gold

Source:www.nigeria.gov.ng/2012-10-29-11-05-46

Every state is endowed with immense mineral and other resources. For example, Japan and some of the other Asian countries hardly started with potentials than most states in Nigeria have. Derivation principle as applied is a veneer under which the federal government perpetrates the fleecing of Nigeria: it is one of lifelines for the Nigeria unitary styled system of government founded upon corruption and injustice. It also helps to sustain an overbearing and uncontrollable bureaucracy that hindered progress while being used as a choice weapon of humiliation and cheating against minorities in Nigeria. Resource control on the other hand, is the magic wand in contemporary economics for empowering and prospering an entire cross section of the socio-economy while promoting individual and property rights contrary to the principle of true federalism.

Not all states have each of the listed minerals in commercial quantities. Those states, having obtained control over their minerals, may form joint mining or exploration ventures with others for mutual benefit. For the purpose of encouraging research, development and mining of regional resource, Development Commissions fashioned after the NDDC but with focus on R & D may be set up in each of the Nigerian geo-political zones. Below is a table showing the key mineral resources in Nigeria:

Table 2:

Key mineral resources in Nigeria

Solid Mineral	Est. Quantity (Metric Tons)	State
Talc	40 million	Niger, Osun, Kogi, Ogun, Kaduna.
Gypsum	1billion +	Nigeria
Iron Ore	3 billion +	Kogi, Enugu, Nigeria FCT
Lead/Zinc centre Nigeria	10 million	East
Barite	8 million+	Taraba, Bauchi
Bentonite	0.7 billion	Nigeria
Gold Western (Alluvial &primary)		South Nigeria
Bitumen	42 billion	Ondo
Coal East centralNigeria	3 billion	Enugu,

Salt springs:		Plateau,Ebonyi	
Rock Salt:	1.5 million+		Benue
Gem Stone:		Plateau, Bauchi	
Sapphire, ruby		Kaduna.	
Aquamarine, emerald,			
Topaz, amethyst, zircon,			
Fluorspar, tourmaline,			
Garnet tourmaline			
Kaolin	3 billion		Nigeria

Source: *Federal Ministry of Solid Mineral Development; Nigeria Coal Corporation, Enugu and CBN surveys.*

It is safe to estimate gross under-capacity mining for each mineral in Table 2. According to the US Geological Survey Minerals Year Book 2005, part of Nigeria production of mineral commodities from 1996 till date is as follows:

Table 3: Mineral production in Nigeria in (Metric/Tons)

Mineral	1996	1997	1998	1999
Kaolin	102,078	100,000	110,000	110,000
Barite	4,000	5,000 est.	200,000	
Gypsum	-	300,000est.	300,000	200,000
Feldspar	-	1,000	500	500
Gold	6	6	10	-
Kilograms)				
Iron and steel	-	-	-	-
Coal, bituminous	7,116	7,000	2,000	2,000
Aluminum	-		2,500 est.	20,000	-
Iron Ore (thsd.Ton)	100	50		

Some data are not available or incomplete due to illegal

mining activities.
Source: US Geological survey Mineral Year Book 2005.

OPINIONS THAT SUGGEST THE PRACTICE OF TRUE FEDERALISM IN NIGERIA

Since the return to civil rule in 1999, a lot of well-meaning Nigerians who have studied the scenario and discovered the predicament of the Nigerian federalism, started

calling for the return to the practice of true federalism in Nigeria. This campaign has been carried out either by individuals, civil society groups, the media, ethnic nationalities, political parties, amongst numerous others, and the campaign is spreading like wild fire because even the North that was not fully awake to the fact is now appreciating the reality of unity in our diversity. Thus, Nigerians are now appreciating the fact that for any meaningful development in unity and progress there must be equity, fairness and justice.

Below are some prominent Nigerians that have lent their voices against the status quo and to canvass for a return to true federalism.

SEN. AHMED BOLA TINUBU

Leading the part of democrats in the quest for the return to the practice of true federalism is Sen. Ahmed Bola Tinubu, a former senator and former Governor of Lagos State and presently, a National Leader of the All Progressives Congress (A.P.C.), the major opposition party in Nigeria today. Tinubu has been at the forefront of those calling for a sovereign National Conference (Just like the one that took place in Ibadan in 1954) comprising of representatives of all the ethnic nationalities, to discuss the way out of the prevailing circumstances.

While presenting a keynote address at a conference with the theme; "Federalism and the Rule of Law," Tinubu, represented by the Governor of Osun State, Comrade Rauf Aregbesola, spoke on the topic "Nigeria Faces Bleak Future without True Federalism." His words, *"until we establish a genuine federalism, we will never achieve our best future. Unless we have real federalism and have it soon, our problems will mount while their solutions* recede. *The Nation in which we live will become a slight and an inferior thing. The way in which we govern ourselves will remain our worst enemy and highest obstacle.*

"The national government should no longer be a powerful Cyclops terrorizing those smaller than it." He pointed out that *"True Federalism is about empowering states and local governments to work for the people they know and who know them. If we can develop this federalism, it will enrich our lives in practical yet profound ways."*

Speaking on the Federal Government's plan to directly fund local government areas, he said. *"It is a political sleight of hand to weaken those state governments controlled by the opposition parties".* He said *"the plan is an attempt to pull the rug from under the opposition state governments by allowing the ruling party in Abuja to gain financial remote control of the local structures that underline state institutions." This is a move towards concentration of power in the federal government and greater concentration of power in one party."*

He said *"the federal plot would make local governments*

beholden to Abuja for its survival. Coordination of economic activities between states and local governments will be over ridden by these federal insertions. Local governments will take directive from Abuja, meaning they would begin to act in cross purposes with their state governments." He suggested a reduction in the power of the central government to avoid having a central government that is too powerful. He said this will countermand constitutional provision *"and disregard established principles of accounting with impunity."*

Tinubu, a man known for his astute belief in the tenets of democratic principles and also a dogged mobilizer for the entrenchment of same, has written books, presented papers and at different fora spoken well to canvass for popular support for the return to the practice of true federalism, by convening a Sovereign National Conference.

GEN. IBRAHIM BADAMOSI BABANGIDA (RTD)

One Nigerian who may have been in the bad books of some Nigerians is Gen. Ibrahim Babangida, mainly because of the singular act of his annulment of the June 12 presidential election in 1993. He has also lent his voice to calls on the Federal Government to take bold steps to ensure that Nigeria is put back on the tracks of true federalism. Babangida, who was military president from 1985 – 1993, has gone back to the drawing board and after a careful study of the Nigerian federalism, discovered that the way out is the return to the practice of true federalism.

Quoted from transparency.com, and speaking on "Nigeria needs true federalism," he said *"I believe that true federalism is the issue of this country."* In nairaland.com, he was quoted as saying *"If my opinion will not be misconstrued again by government spin doctors and naysayers, I would rather call on President Goodluck Jonathan to seize the moment by legitimately embarking on complete restructuring of the country in order to put into practice the real principles of federalism. There is too much power concentration at the centre, thus, weakening the comparative abilities of the federating units at generating wealth for their constituents. History will be kind on Mr. President if he takes this bold step at ensuring the practice of true federalism. My very honest advice is that President Goodluck should commence the process of devolving powers from the centre to the federating units, states and local governments, in order to gain sufficient time and concentration on several other development issues that would help make the nation move forward.* He said *"Let me reiterate the strong need for Mr. President to commence the process of practicing fiscal federalism in the area of power devolution, anti-corruption crusade, attitudinal reorientation, bureaucratic reforms, slim government, unicameral legislature and transparency in governance."*

AHMED JODA

Ahmed Joda, who is chairman of the Nigerian Communications Commission (NCC), also spoke in support of the return to the practice of true federalism. Speaking on the topic "the State of the Nigerian Nation" at the ceremony of the award of the Leadership Governor of the year by the LEADERSHIP newspapers in Abuja, he said *"our country has passed through difficult times, including a civil war and has survived. We must not mistake the fact of our survival to anything such as military might. The truth is that we have survived because the ordinary Nigerian overwhelmingly desires to live together in one united country under some commonly acceptable arrangement. It is quite clear from all we are passing through and from all the political debates in which we have been engaged, that there is a sufficient body of opinion around the country that the present arrangements are not adequate and need to be discussed further."*

ALHAJI ATIKU ABUBAKAR

Former Vice President, Alhaji Atiku Abubakar has also called for a return to the practice of true federalism in Nigeria. In his opening remarks as the chairman of the 2012 leadership conference and awards ceremony in Abuja on Tuesday, September 18th, 2012, he called for the overhauling of the Nigerian political structure in order to pave way for true federalism. He also publicly regretted not supporting former Vice-President Alex Ekwueme's call for the creation of six semi-autonomous federal regions. He said *"now I realize that I should have supported him because our current federal structure is clearly not working. Dr. Ekwueme obviously saw what some of us with our civil war mindset could not see at the time. There is indeed too much concentration of power and resources at the centre. And it is stifling our march to true greatness as a nation and threatening our unity because of all the abuse, inefficiencies, corruption and reactive tensions that it has been generating"*. He further confirmed that *"one of the consequences of excessive centralization and the military rule that facilitated it is that it made the Nigerian President the most powerful President in the world. This is because he could quite literally unleash all security agencies on an individual or organization, undermine the National Assembly, and turn the Judiciary into an almost pro-government and conformist organ.*

"The excessive powers bestowed on the President of the country must be taken away because government has lost its capacity to carry responsibilities effectively. It has stretched its strength limit and our priority should be in

changing the federal structure. He said decentralization is not an invitation to the breakup of the country and national unity. Nigerians should not be confused with unitary and concentration of power and resources at the federal level.

"It is sad to note also that fifty two years after independence, the country's political system is still in a downward spiral with no redemption in sight. We may soon reach a point where the citizens no longer have faith in the system's ability to serve them.

"There is indeed too much concentration of power and resources at the centre. It is stifling our march to true greatness as a nation and threatening our unity because of all the abuses, inefficiencies, corruption and reactive tensions that it has been generating." There is need, therefore, to review the structure of the Nigerian federation, preferably along the basis of the current six geo-political zones as regions and the states as provinces. The existing states structure may not suffice, as the states are too weak materially and politically to provide what is needed for good governance."

DR. ALEX EKWUEME

One detribalized Nigerian who stands as an icon of unity and one of the leading proponents for the return to the practice of true federalism is Dr. Alex Ekwueme, the former Vice President of the Second Republic. He recently turned eighty (80) years and many people have been pouring encomiums on him in recognition of his exemplary leadership and great ideas.

Dr. Alex Ekwueme has been passionate about the unity of Nigeria in its diversity. This, he suggested, can only be achieved through the practice of true federalism. At the Constitutional Conference of 1995, he suggested that power should be decentralized and the six geo-political zones should be the administrative centers as semi-autonomous federal regions. His ideas were not considered by some Nigerians to be the solution to the Nigerian structural decay as at the time until recent unfolding events have proved him right.

ALHAJI BALARABE MUSA

Alhaji Balarabe Musa, former civilian governor of old Kaduna State, is chairman of the People's Redemption Party (PRP) and leader of the Conference of Nigeria Political Parties (CNPP). In an interview with OBIRE ONAKEMU, he spoke on the state of the nation. As a Northerner and a former governor, when he was asked his position on resource control and true federalism, he commented that; *"I am in support of true federalism, in the sense that federated units should be capable of taking care of some responsibilities, for instance, education. But if true federalism means making the federal government weaker than it is now, particularly with the serious problems we have with uneven development and insecurity, then I need a second thought.*

But definitely, I support true federalism in the sense of making the federal government take less than what it is taking now from the federation account. The President is too powerful, just like the governors, who are equally powerful. Their powers in the constitution should be reduced. The money going to the federal government should be substantially reduced in favor of more going to the local governments; but a better alternative is for the federating units to be regions rather than the 36 states and Abuja.

There is every need for us to have constitutional amendments, while states and the local governments should be reduced to six or eight regions. And each region could establish as many states and local governments that they can cope with on the basis of what is allocated to them federally and the internally generated revenues that are available to them.

In other words, this can be interpreted to mean 6-8 zones or regions to replace the 36 states and Abuja and the 774 Local governments. If that should be the case, then, what goes to the federal government should be reduced in favor of more going to the states and local governments. At the moment I think about 50 percent goes to the federal government; it should now be limited to about 35 percent and the rest should go to about six or eight regions."

Question: What happens if the idea of regionalism fails to fly with the political class?

But if we cannot return to the former arrangement of

regions and we must continue with the 36 states, Abuja as FCT and 774 local governments, then, we need to reduce the power of the President substantially and equally the power of state governors and make more funds available to the local government councils.

Question: Some Nigerians have called for a national conference and others call it sovereign national conference. Which one do you canvass?

As far as I am concerned, the best is a sovereign national conference. But if those of us asking for it are not united on the issue, then, let us have a national conference. I know a sovereign national conference has the implications of establishing another reality of replacing this government and throwing in another reality. I am not afraid of that! I am not even afraid of the way to get it! But I want to make sure that Nigerians are prepared for it. If Nigerians are not prepared for it, then let us have a national conference.

But I am opposed to a national conference based on ethnic nationalities. I think it is very unnecessary at the moment;

we have matured far above that in spite of our problems. Let us have a fresh national conference based on citizenship".

In the wake of the onslaught of military dictatorship till the present dispensation, different pressure groups emerged, particularly in the southern part of Nigeria to demand for the convening of a Sovereign National Conference where the Nigerian federalism should be laid on the table for diagnosis of the ailments besetting her so as to administer the right kind of medication – obviously true federalism, still remains the viable options and it shall always be as long as the diversities inherent in the polity still persist and if at all any meaningful progress is hoped to be achieved.

The American model is one of several others that can be studied and applied as found in en.wikipedia.org/Americanfederalism which stated that "Federalism and the Federal system define the basic structure of American government. There were many disagreements at the constitutional convention. Many delegates feared a national government that was too strong and many delegates feared that state's rights would merely continue the weak form of government under the articles. The constitution created a federal system of government (Federalism) as a compromise.

Under federalism, power is shared and decided between national and state governments. Each has specific powers unto itself while they also share certain powers. Both levels have their own agencies and officials and directly affect the people. The founding fathers really had no other choice except federalism. The weak union created under the articles would not work, yet people did not want to give all the power to a national government. Federalism was the middle ground... compromise.... a way to distribute authority between the states and the national government."

That was a similar situation where the nationalists found themselves at the eve of independence and thus, came to a compromise because there was no any other choice but federalism. This heralded the birth of the independence constitution which was used to administer the affairs of the nation till January, 1966 when it was aborted.

Therefore, in disagreement with the proponents of a sovereign National Conference especially in this democratic dispensation, it is better to convene National Conference where all the issues of Nigerian dwindling federalism would be discussed and solutions found.

When General Olusegun Obasanjo (rtd) became president for the second time in 1999, the document used during the Second Republic (1979 Constitution) was unearthed and renamed the 1999 Constitution which has since been implemented till date instead of reflecting on the nation's past history and picking the missing links to make amends. There was nothing fundamentally wrong with the independence constitution except for the political impasse that needed a political will to be mustered to address such. In this regards, if Nigeria has to make any headway, then that document has to be brought out from the archives, studied and applied after due amendments and relevant (necessary) additions are made to it. Just as K.C Wheare rightly observed, one of the conditions precedent to the existence of a federal arrangement is a force of imitation that is, the prior existence of a federal constitution to serve as a model.

For the recent quagmire that has arisen and is generating so much debate in the polity, which is the question of whether there is need for a state police in Nigeria or not, so many Nigerians have argued for and others against the creation of state police in Nigeria. However, it all depends on how one looks at it. But the fact is that there is need for local policing to effectively deal with the issues of crime and criminality, especially the issues of insurgencies by local militia usually connected to outside forces, the rise and prevalence of various sects that unleash terror on innocent citizens and the proliferation of both small and large arms and ammunition often used by these groups. To effectively deal with such issues to a large extent, there should be a state police in place. The fact cannot be overemphasized of the American example where state police has been operating successfully – some large institutions separately run their internal security systems for effectiveness. These are models where the Nigerian system can emulate.

True federalism, instead of what is now in place, should create the platform for the control of the police force by the various states governors who are always constraint when it comes to prompt deployment of forces to quell or to unravel the mysteries behind crime and criminality, since the forces, located in the states are controlled from the centre. Devolution of powers in essence to the states should include the powers to run state owned police force.

One area of major contention is the fact that state governors usually in crisis ridden areas sometimes have running battles with the central government in the issue of deployment of forces to quell such crisis in times of dire need. An example is the Jos Plateau State series of crisis, where the state Governor cannot order the deployment of forces without instruction from the headquarters as required by law.

In the words of Governor Jonah David Jang of Plateau state;

"We are running a federation in Nigeria; that is why we

are called the Federal Republic of Nigeria. In fact, higher institutions like Universities have their own police and Nigeria, the biggest black nation in the world has a central police system...as Governor of a state, with constitutional powers to be the chief security officer of the state, I cannot 'command even a fly'...Most times my decisions were not followed by security operatives after meeting with the state security council, because they had to take orders from their bosses...A typical example was when the Plateau crisis started in 2008;we arrested 250 people from Niger and Chad and we were then investigating them. Suddenly, they were taken to Abuja to be investigated in Abuja and we never saw them again.

"This development negates the constitution of the country which states that an alleged criminal should be investigated and tried where he committed the offence. But this is not happening in Nigeria because of the system of security we have....The creation of state police would also ensure better training and performance of police personnel in the country...We believe that states should be able to run their own police force. The Nigeria police are *like civil servants, people join the service and rise through the ranks and they are not trained. If states have their own police, training will be organized at that level and the police will be better trained and equipped...The military was brought to douse tension in crisis prone states because the police could not wake up to its own responsibility."*

In his own submission, former Deputy Speaker of the Plateau State House of Assembly, Hon. John Bull Shekarau, who doubled as Chairman, Peace and Reconciliation Committee, observed that;

"The violence in the state and in the country is getting to its climax. Is the Federal Government just there to supervise the killing of its citizens every day? We have resolved as a House that this President owes us explanation and he should tell Nigerians what is going on. We have also resolved that this House is demanding for a state police because it is obvious that the Federal police are failing. We are also demanding immediate removal of soldiers from the streets of Plateau and the return of responsibilities of securing citizens to the Governor who is

the chief security officer of the state."

Former Plateau State Commissioner of Police, CP Emmanuel Oladipo Ayeni, now retired, on his last day in office, publicly expressed his own insider views on the system that continues to ridicule the force and renders it ineffective, having witnessed so much grief and pain of the people he was posted to secure. He said;

"The state of the Nigeria Police Force is worrisome. The personnel of the Police do not have necessary logistics to work within all the states of the country. There are no sufficient vehicles to perform our statutory duties of protection of lives and property, maintenance of law and order, apprehension of offenders and enforcement of all laws with which the force is directly charged.

"Virtually all the state police commands rely on the assistance of State Governments for provision of vehicles, communications and necessary logistics. I came to Plateau State on July 11th, 2011; a state that is facing serious security challenges. No single vehicle has been given to the command by the Federal Government. Apart from that, a single liter of fuel has not been given to the command as well. How does the Federal Government want the Police to function and perform its statutory duties under this type of climate? If not for assistance

from the State Government, everything would have collapsed."

"Therefore, if the problem of security challenges must be solved, the Federal Government must take the issue of security serious by giving the Nigerian police the attention it deserves. If this is not done, there will be increased criminal activities in the country while the police watch helplessly. The Federal Government must wake up and play its constitutional role of providing security in the country."

Consequent upon the above, he also supported the clarion call for state police to be in place when he stated that; *"The ongoing agitation for state police is in order. There is no single Federation in the world apart from Nigeria where police is controlled by the central Government alone. Put differently, having police at all levels of Government is the hallmark of a Federal system of Government. Even under the 1963 Republican Constitution in Nigeria, there were the Nigerian Police at the Center, Native Authority Police in the Northern Region and Local Government Police in the Southern Region of*

Nigeria. That apart, with the inability of the Federal Government to properly fund the police as highlighted above the need for state police cannot be overemphasized."

CHAPTER NINE

VISIONARY AND INCORRUPTIBLE LEADERSHIP

Vision is the ability to see what things could be in the future rather than what things are. Visionary leaders, on their own part, have the ability to see what things could be in the future rather than what things are. Through the attractive visions that they have, they are able to attract followers to themselves which enable them to plan for their people in the future. One very great visionary leader who happens to be my mentor is Bishop David Oyedepo. In one of his inspiring messages, he said that *''if a person does not know where he is going to, then anywhere will look like it.''* However, having had the vision, a leader must be able to share his vision with his people since leadership is influencing others toward a common goal. When people see that by working together they can create a more ideal future, they will give more of themselves in achieving the cause and their heart is won to the course and vision of their leader if they understand it to be genuine. Leaders have a great talent in seeing potentials in every situation. They don't see what things are, but what things could be. Leadership should not only be visionary but incorruptible.

Events in the recent political history of Nigeria have proved that good leadership (visionary and incorruptible) is not necessarily embedded in any political affiliation, religious belief or geo-political background. The legend, Martin Luther King Junior, in his epochal speech about segregation of other races by the whites said that "a time shall come when my four little children shall not be judged by the color of their skin, but by the content of their character". It is also the case in Nigeria today that in the near future, leaders will not be chosen by the religious belief they belong to, the political party they have affiliation with, the ethnic group they belong to or the geo-political location they come from, but leaders shall be elected based on the content of their characters.

Examples of leaders who have motivated their followers and brought great development to their country include:

NELSON MANDELA

He was the first black President of South Africa and was one of the most influential freedom fighters of apartheid in South Africa. After tenure as president, he refused to contest for another term and went on to become an advocate for a variety of social and human rights organizations.

BISHOP DAVID OYEDEPO

Through his visionary leadership, Bishop David Oyedepo has been able to inspire millions of Nigerians and Africans who were previously living in penury into untold abundance, through his teachings on the biblical kind of wisdom that gives hope. He runs a well-organized church and educational network around the world that can be emulated by the secular community.

MARTIN LUTHER KING (Jnr.)

An American Baptist preacher, an activist and prominent leader in American Civil Right Movement, his greatest work was to fight for the rights of African Americans. He adopted the method of Ghandi.

LEE KUAN YEW

He was the first and longest serving Prime Minister of Singapore; and it was his leadership that brought third world Singapore into a thriving metropolitan city in a stunning three decades which is attracting educationists and industrialists from all over the world.

LATE SHEHU MUSA YAR'ADUA

The soft spoken former President of the Federal Republic of Nigeria, late Alhaji Shehu Musa Yar'adua was a focused visionary and incorruptible leader. He was the first Nigerian President to publicly declare his assets which indicated that after serving as Governor of Katsina State for two tenures of four years each, he was worth next to nothing compared to his fellow Governors who probably had money stashed away in foreign banks.

His policies, the seven point agenda geared towards transforming the entire nation, was a masterpiece which sadly came to a regrettable end after his death. Ill-health stood in the way of his full implementation of the Agenda. He was a president Nigeria never had the opportunity to fully enjoy.

OUR FOUNDING FATHERS

Our leaders that fought for the independence of Nigeria and later drafted the independence constitution were all visionary leaders that were selflessly patriotic. They saw the need for Nigerians to become self-governing and did all they could to obtain that from the colonialists. They also were able to see the kind of administrative structure that best suits the Nigerian nation and worked towards tailoring a federalist constitution that was and is still adjudged the best constitution to govern the divergent ethnic nationalities in Nigeria. Our founding fathers did a great job by laying a foundation that has not been built upon.

PASTOR SAM ADEYEMI

Pastor Sam Adeyemi is the Senior Pastor at the Daystar Christian Centre who also presents the programme 'Success Power' on both television and radio. He organizes a programme tagged: *"Excellence in Leadership Conference"*, every year. He saw the rot in government circles and realized that leaders gain access to position of authority without obtaining the necessary and relevant training as to how to handle the issues of corruption and corrupt practices and other exigencies of office. This programme is aimed at training leaders in all sectors of the Nigerian economy and politics to prepare them for the challenges that are ahead. It was at one of such conferences that the inspiration to write this book was born.

GEN. MOHAMMADU BUHARI (RTD)

A former head of State and a two time presidential candidate in the All Nigeria Peoples Party and the Congress for Progressive change, Gen. Mohammadu Buhari (rtd), is another visionary and incorruptible leader. His military administration introduced a culture of discipline in the system before it was terminated. He is known to be one leader who does not corruptly enrich himself while holding any public office entrusted to him. However, religious issues stand as an impediment against his aspirations.

In the book "The Trouble with Nigeria" by Chinua Achebe, he said, "The trouble with Nigeria is simply and squarely a failure of leadership. There is nothing wrong with Nigeria's land, climate, water, air or anything else. The Nigerian problem is the unwillingness or inability of its leaders to rise to the responsibility, or to the challenge with personal examples, which is the hallmark of true leadership. Nigeria can change today, if she discovers leaders who have the will, ability and the vision."

CHAPTER TEN

CREDIBLE (FREE AND FAIR) POLLS

The conduct of free and fair election is not negotiable in any democratic setting to ensure stability, peace, unity and progress. The institution in charge of the conduct of elections in Nigeria today is the Independent National Electoral Commission (INEC). The history of Election Management Bodies in Nigeria dates back to the colonial era, with the establishment of the then Electoral Commission of Nigeria (ECN) to conduct the 1959 pre-independence general elections.

At independence, Nigeria under the Abubakar Tafewa Balewa administration set up the Federal Electoral Commission (FEC) to conduct the 1964 and 1965 regional elections. Following the political crises which led to the military coup d'etat of 1966, the electoral commission was dissolved. In 1978, the military administration of General Olusegun Obasanjo established a new Federal Electoral Commission (FEDECO). It conducted the 1979 transitional elections which ushered in Nigeria's Second Republic with Alhaji Shehu Shagari as President. FEDECO was again dissolved when the civilian administration was overthrown by the military led by General Muhammadu

Buhari on December 31, 1983. In 1987, the General Ibrahim Babangida regime that took over from General Buhari set up the National Electoral Commission (NEC). The Commission commenced the implementation of a transition programme which was however, aborted as a result of the June 12 1993 crisis.

On November 17, 1993, General Sani Abacha who took over as head of State dissolved NEC and replaced it in 1995 with the National Electoral Commission (NECON). With the death of General Sani Abacha in 1998, his successor, General Abdulsalami Abubakar established the Independent National Electoral Commission (INEC) by Decree No. 17 of 1998 which is now an act of the National Assembly.

FUNCTIONS OF THE COMMISSION

The responsibilities of the Commission are to:

1.   Organize, undertake and supervise all elections to the offices of the President and Vice President, the Governor and Deputy Governor of a State and to the membership of the Senate, the House of Representatives and the House of Assembly of each state of the federation.
2.   Register political parties in accordance with the provisions of the Constitution of the Federal Republic of Nigeria (1979) and an act of the National Assembly; monitor the organization and operation of political parties including their finances.
3.   Arrange for the annual examination and auditing of

4. funds and accounts of political parties and publish a report on such examination and audit for public information.
5. Arrange and conduct the registration of persons qualified to vote and prepare, maintain and revise the register of voters for the purpose of any election under the constitution.
6. Delimit and delineate constituencies.
7. Monitor political campaigns and provide rules and regulations which shall govern political parties.
8. Ensure that all Electoral Commissioners, Electoral and Returning Officers take and subscribe to the oath of office prescribed by law.
9. Delegate any of its powers to any Resident Electoral Commissioner; and,
10. Carry out such other functions as may be conferred upon it by an Act of the National Assembly.

The conduct of elections is the primary responsibility of the Election Management bodies including the one in existence today (INEC). However, the conduct of a credible free and fair election is one of the panaceas to the threats to the corporate existence of Nigeria by 2015.

As captured by the late Dr. Festus Iyayi, to a very large extent, elections and electoral practices shape the fate of the bourgeois modern nation state. Elections provide the medium by which the different interest groups within the bourgeois nation state can stake and resolve their claims to power through peaceful means.

Elections, therefore, determine the manner and methods by which changes in the bourgeois social order may be brought about.

Where elections fail to validly arbitrate between competing political claims, individuals and groups may be left to their own means including assassinations, coup d'etat, revolutions, insurgency and bush wars to press their claim to power. An example of these is the 1965 elections that were said to be controversial and were largely responsible for the coup d'etat of 1966.

The flawed elections of 1983 were used as the rationale for the military coup of December 31st 1983. Likewise the Babangida flawed elections of 1993 produced the Abacha palace coup of that year which paved way to his memorable dictatorship.

As we approach 2015, it is apparent to all Nigerians that the general elections will not only determine the survival of Nigeria as a Nation but also the survival of democracy in the country.

Some of the chronic problems of elections in Nigeria include;
(i)   Ethnic rivalries
(ii)   Religious differences
(iii)   Foreign interference
(iv)   The problem of oil
(v)   The character of the Nigerian state
(vi)   The nature of the political class

(vii)   The role and performance of INEC.

PROBLEMS ASSOCIATED WITH THE CONDUCT OF ELECTIONS SINCE INDEPENDENCE

Nigeria's electoral history has not been a pleasant one. Since attainment of independence in 1960, Nigeria has been bedeviled by political instability fueled largely by an electoral process in crisis.

The country and her leaders failed to learn from history and avoid the past mistakes in order to pave the way for a secure political process, thus the mistakes of the past have been perpetuated. These are characterized by ugly incidences of political thuggery and violence, electoral malpractice both at political parties primaries level and general elections, unending lawsuits, crisis of legitimacy, instability and chaos.

Over the period of Nigeria's existence as an independent nation-state, all these negative attributes of her political processes have often provided compelling reasons for military adventurists to seize power from its alleged civilian collaborators.

The 1964/65 elections were characterized by widespread rigging, intimidation and chaos that led to the boycott of the polls which later created serious constitutional dilemma. The later election of the western region was marred by massive rigging and other irregularities and widespread violence.

The 1979 elections that brought in Shehu Shagari to power were criticized by international observers as having been widely rigged. The 1983 election was said to have been marred by corruption, political violence and polling irregularities. The 1997, 2003 and 2007 elections were lampooned by many critics as far from free and fair. The 2007 election, in particular, was described as the worst in the history of the nation because of indescribable irregularities which marred the elections.

However, the 1993 and 2011 elections were adjudged to be the freest and fairest in the history of elections since independence. While the 1993 election was later annulled, the consequences that followed that decision almost cost the nation her unity. In this regard, the INEC as presently constituted, organized and conducted the 2011 general elections; thus, marked improvements should be made on the past achievements.

FACTORS THAT CAN ENHANCE THE PERFORMANCE OF INEC IN THE CONDUCT OF CREDIBLE ELECTIONS

Having identified the problems associated with the conduct of elections in Nigeria since independence, a lot of factors can come in handy to enhance the performance of INEC in the conduct of credible elections.

First of all, the action plan for the conduct of the 2015 general elections should be guided by the vision and mission statements of the commission.

The mission statement of the commission says;
"The mission of the Independent National Electoral Commission (INEC) is to provide credible and efficient electoral services consistent with the principles of equity, justice and fair play for the building of a strong and viable democracy in Nigeria."

While the vision statement states that;
"The vision of the Independent National Electoral Commission (INEC) is that of a dynamic, formidable and independent organization, committed to the institutionalization of an enduring democracy, which allows for effective and smooth political change." There are eight guiding principles formulated to enable the commission to fulfill its vision and mission, which are:

AUTONOMY: Relentless in the pursuit of autonomy for effective electoral services.

TRANSPARENCY: Openness in all activities and in relation with stakeholders, the media service providers and the people of Nigeria.

INTEGRITY: Demonstration of high moral standards and honesty in all dealings with the people of Nigeria.

CREDIBILITY: Credibility in all actions and activities, thereby remaining an institution that people can trust.

IMPARTIALITY: Creation of a level playing field for all political actors.

DEDICATION: Commitment to providing quality electoral services for the people of Nigeria.

EQUITY: Fairness and justice in dealing with all people and,

EXCELLENCE: Promotion of excellence and ensuring that merit remains the basis for the recruitment and compensation of staff.

Thus, in line with the guiding principles to the vision and mission statements of the commission, the following factors are crucial to the success of the 2015 general elections.

(i)   **ELECTORAL AND CONSTITUTIONAL REFORMS**.
The need for fundamental structural changes by way of Electoral and constitutional reforms has been identified as a necessary prerequisite for achieving a credible and sustainable electoral process. Having identified the lapses in the Electoral Act 2010, the commission as presently constituted is working towards achieving this which has to follow a process.
(a)   Drafting of amendments to the Electoral Act 2010.
(b)   Drafting of suggested amendments to the Constitution of the Federal Republic of Nigeria.
(c)   Submission of draft bill to stakeholders.
(d)   Presentation of the final draft Electoral Bill to the National Assembly.

However, the timely passage of all such bills by the National Assembly shall enhance the level of success of the general elections.

(ii) CAPACITY BUILDING OF ELECTORAL MANAGEMENT STAFF

As part of restructuring of INEC to be knowledge based organization capable of repositioning the commission for conducting elections in the 21st Century, "The Electoral Institute" was established in 2005. It consists of three departments namely; Training, Voter Education and Research & Documentation. It has centres in Ibadan, Nsukka, Zaria, Nassarawa and Oghara. The commission has been organizing training, workshops and seminars to boost staff capacity and knowledge as they prepare for the forthcoming polls.

(iii) SUSTAINED VOTER EDUCATION AND PUBLIC ENLIGHTENMENT

To achieve the goal of conducting free and fair poll in the nation, it is imperative to have an enlightened and politically sophisticated citizenry with the capacity to make informed choices at elections; choices that would confer legitimacy to elected representatives and executives.

The current approach to voter education (enlightenment) that is being carried out through the electronic and print media, as well as alternative or non-formal channels like the shareholders forum, is intended to create a level playing field such that popular political participation would be seen as having flowed from the people. The recent merging together of the Public Affairs Department and the Voter Education Department of the Electoral Institute has added impetus to this campaign.

(iv)   COMPILATION OF A VALID VOTER REGISTER

The register of voters, the world over is the acceptable minimum requirement for ensuring free and fair elections in liberal democratic societies. Election management bodies in the past have tried with little success to compile national voters' rolls that could meet the above stated requirement.

All these efforts fall short of expectation as they were always criticized of not being accurate or credible They were marred by double registration under aged registrants etc. Dr. Abel Guobadia's OMR approach also fell far short of expectation. With the application of a modern technology (ICT) to the election process, the INEC, under Professor Maurice Iwu, introduced Direct Data Capture (DDC) machines which were deployed for the 2006/2007 registration exercise. However, the 2007 general elections were not any better because it was discovered that the register of voters contained photographs of clearly under aged voters, of Mike Tyson and of the father of post-apartheid South Africa, the late Nelson Mandela were found in the register.

At the onset of the new commission with Prof. Attahiru Jega at the helm of affairs, the voters register was conducted despite time constraint and DDC machines were deployed to cover the 120,000 polling units across the nation. The commission developed in house software that facilitated the capture of ten finger prints of registrants, apart from other details such as gender, age, address and photographs. A more effective run of the Automated finger print identification system (AFIS) was done on the data captured during the voter registration exercise, resulting to the discovery of over 870,000 double or multiple registrations which were consequently weeded out of the register. This and other factors resulted in the success witnessed in 2011.

A continuous registration exercise has been slated to cater for those who had turned 18 years after the conduct of the last exercise in January, 2011; those who transferred their registration after changing residence, those whose biometrics could not be captured during the last exercise and those whose biometrics were captured but their photographs did not appear on the emergent electronic voters register. Prospective registrants are expected to present such evidence as birth or baptismal certificates, national passports, identity card or driver's license or any other document that will prove the identity, age and nationality of the applicant. This contributed significantly in forestalling all forms of registration frauds during the continuous registration process in the states where the exercise preceded the Governorship elections that took place there.

According to the Chairman, Prof. Attahiru Jega, "the Electronic Voter Register now in place is a national voter's roll which is not only comprehensive, accurate and reliable but also all-inclusive." He further disclosed that "the chip based voter cards have been configured to last for ten years while card readers which will hopefully be deployed during the 2015 general elections, would be part of the integrated system INEC intends to deploy to ensure rig-proof elections in the future."

(v) ROLE OF POLITICAL PARTIES

Political parties are one of the core stakeholders in the process that leads to the conduct of general elections. For a general election to be free and fair and free of rancor, the process by which political parties adopt to present their flag bearers for any elective post should be seen to be transparent. Imposition of candidates has been a recurring complains emanating from political parties over time. This has always had a negative impact on the general election as the allegedly imposed candidates at primaries will always want to rig their way into public office since there was no popular support in the first place. Political parties, therefore, should work towards preserving our nascent democratic heritage.

(iv) SECURITY

Having all the above in place, it is imperative to have security in place during every election. Adequate security must be in place to forestall election malpractices. Past efforts should be improved upon.

In conclusion, from all indications, the INEC has worked and is still working tirelessly to ensure a credible free and fair 2015 elections. However, staff enhanced welfare should be considered as paramount to help boost their

moral in conducting an election that means everything to
all of us.

CHAPTER ELEVEN

THE NIGERIAN SPIRIT: ORIENTATION AND REORIENTATION

Many Nigerians lost faith in the project of Nigeria because there is no proper awareness and the majority of the people are not carried along. As far as majority of the citizens are concerned, the term 'Nigeria' only exists on paper and not in reality. Instead of seeing themselves as Nigerians, they see themselves as Northerners, South-Westerners, South-Southerners, South Easterners or Middle-Belters, or belonging to one ethnic group or the other or a part of a particular religion. Some lean more to their political affiliations. There is no cohesion among the divergence of ethnic nationalities. Thus, there is need to inculcate the culture of creating awareness among the divergent groups about the importance of first seeing themselves as Nigerians before any other affiliation, be it regional, ethnic, religious or political. In the Nigerian project, there is need to re-orientate the people on the words of the Nigerian national anthem and the Pledge.

Millions of Nigerians today who are adults cannot recite the National Anthem or the Pledge; and therefore do not have any working knowledge of what is in it.

A ministerial nominee, while undergoing screening at the Senate was asked to recite the national anthem but could not do so and yet was asked to take a bow and leave and was later confirmed as a Minister. How can such a person minister unto the needs of millions of Nigerians who do not also have the mental picture of the Nigerian dream?

Even in schools today, where the national anthem and the pledge are recited, such is done absent mindedly like any other song that is sang and forgotten immediately the last word is said. With regard to these developments, there is need to teach on the real meaning of the National Anthem and the Pledge in schools. It is necessary for the media both, print and electronic, to massively begin to create this awareness among the people, so that a "Nigerian spirit" can be projected in the minds of all. Knowledge, they say is, power.

The creation of a positive mindset among the populace is what the nation has to vigorously start to pursue in order to change citizens perception of the nation. This could be achieved through a massive all out nationwide campaign aimed at projecting the positive image of the nation vis-à-vis the enormous potentials that lay both within the human and national resources in Nigeria. This could be done in multiple dimensions.

First is to launch a nationwide media campaign through all the media outlets to project the image of the nation, enlightening citizens on the paramount goal of seeing themselves first as Nigerians before any other affiliations whether ethnic, regional, and religious.

There should also be a carefully scripted agenda to infuse every Nigerian with the mindset of possibility thinking. Mindsets have a powerful effect on action and behavior which is widely recognized. Our mindsets determine how we think, talk and behave. They are more powerful than structures or systems, and they forge the set of individual or collective beliefs and assumptions that guide people at all levels in what they have to do in order to succeed internally and externally.

Secondly is to also include this mindset transformation agenda into the nation's academic curriculum. Youngsters should be infused with the positive mentality of the fact that in Nigeria nothing is impossible and an unrepentant belief in the workability of the Nigerian state. There is need to inculcate national pride in the minds of pupils and students in both post primary and tertiary levels.

Civil education was recently introduced in national school curriculum. This could be beefed up with a programme of changing all the negative perceptions about the nation by working on the mindsets wrongly created in the past replacing them with powerful positive national views.

Nigerian politicians also need to change their mindsets about how they view the nation at large in their bid to wrest power and other political manipulations. It is imperative to realize that in all their permutations and quest to appropriate power, national interest comes first before any other individual or group interest. A sense of national interest embedded in the hearts of politicians and the general public will naturally neutralize any hard stance about who gets what, when and how it can be acquired.

In changing mindsets, politicians and other citizens can first and foremost have the desire to change, and then make a decision to change, then the actions mandated by such decisions must be deployed.

Finally, they should determine to sustain such actions, practices and behaviors required.

The words of our National Anthem are just as the morning devotion we do every day which must first be impressed on our spirits before they can find expression in our lives. America is a country Nigeria can choose to emulate. They sing their national anthem with their spirit, soul and body which make them believe in it and thus creating the desire in them to work for the common interest of AMERICA.

By making the spirit of the national anthem to be impressed on our spirits, Nigerians will automatically develop the love for their country and for fellow citizens of the country. Hence, love conquers all challenges because it never fails. The bible in 1Corinthians 13 (KJV) speaks on the subject of love and it emphasizes that love is the greatest.

Whatever cause you are fighting or organization you are leading, it's good to know that ultimately, above all else, it is love that can change the world. Your methods and strategies can get you far but it is the love for the people that will drive you to achieve what you set out to do. The Nigerian popular musician TUFACE IDIBIA in his song ONE LOVE, said that, *"all we need is love, irrespective of our color, our religious or political border."* Martin Luther King

Junior said *"Love is the only force capable of transforming an enemy into friend"*. He also said *"darkness cannot drive out darkness, only light can do that, hate cannot drive out hate only love can do that."* The bible in the book of John Chapter 1 verse 5 (KJV) says, and the light shinned in darkness and the darkness comprehended it not. Love is that light Nigeria needs to make a true difference in every aspect of life including its national affairs. The sage, Mahatma Ghandi was one leader that put this theory into practical reality in the political arena when he inspired millions of people to stage a non-violent revolution through his popular SATYA GRAHA (the force of truth and love) and AHIMSA (non-violence to all living things).

By projecting the Nigerian dream on the minds of all Nigerians, the issues of ethnicity and religious bigotry will now be reduced to its barest minimum. If these indices are embraced by Nigerians political parties can now develop into truly national parties with sincere membership cutting across the thirty six states of the federation thus integrating into numerous ethnic nationalities and winning the confidence of all the religious beliefs.

Ghana has experimented with this by floating a political party that is nationalist in outlook with membership cutting across the country and this has brought stability to the country. This can further be boosted when the scourge of economic deprivation is addressed and Nigerians now have unrestricted access to their commonwealth. Even corruption of greed that has become the order of the day will now become a thing of the past. Nigerians will now have a common sense of nationhood. Thus, pilfering of public assets will gradually be reduced to the barest minimum from the Nigerian national life. Also, by having a culture of nationhood restored in the polity, insecurity shall also be dealt with by the citizens themselves. A sense of nationhood will project a culture of being our brother's keepers and thus acting to protect each other from harm or deprivation. By having a spirit of our own, Nigerians can and will be able to free ourselves from the shackles of western interest in political and economic affairs.

The fact is that the difference between developed

nations and under developed nations is not natural resources or infrastructure. It is rather a carefully and powerfully scripted perception of nationhood. Johnson Abbally in his book, **unleashed**, rightly stated that *"Americans perceive America as the land of the brave and free. And they seduce the rest of the world to think the same way of America. Every tenet, every action, every creed, every endeavor, indeed, everything Americans do, they do with bold audacity because they believe themselves to be mentally capable and absolutely free to explore new frontiers of possibilities. That perception is not an evolutionary accident. It is a carefully scripted systematic propaganda aimed at infusing every new born there with the mindset that in America nothing is impossible."*

Above all else, prayer is the key to the realms of unlimited possibilities. It carries a force that is capable of transforming a nation from retardation to development. America has been able to attain and retain her position as the world's most powerful nation as a result of prayer warriors who intercede for the nation. In the early days of the American republic, a stranger once asked a congressman how he could distinguish George Washington. He was told, "You can easily distinguish him when congress goes to pray. Washington is the gentleman who knees."

A curse was laid on the American presidency by the red Indians which run down the generations when American presidents were assassinated after every ten years. This was beginning to affect the nation adversely because all the good programmes of such leaders were being cut down by the assailants' bullets. The realization of this made America to call for a National Prayer Conference to avert the curse. Today, Americans are enjoying the fruits of a committed prayer life. Jesus told us that "men ought always to pray and not to faint" – Luke 18:1.

An open door has been set before us that no man can shut; therefore Nigerians should walk into it and possess our possessions.

CONCLUSION

In conclusion, it is pertinent to note that Nigeria has come to a cross-road. Urgent and necessary steps have to be put in place so as to salvage the nation from the impending collapse that is looming. True federalism will open up the country to a competitive economic diversification whereby all resources will be exploited and channeled towards catering for the welfare of all Nigerians.

Next to this is the need for capable leadership to be in place. Ethnicity and religious bigotry have been the greatest undoings which have robbed the nation of competent leadership. The true value of any candidate is in his/her character and the ability to deliver on promises made to the electorate. Religion is a personal affair between man and God and should, therefore, be separated from political campaigns. Nigerians should shun ethnic and religious bigots and vote for people who can lead well and translate their dreams and aspirations into reality. Most of the developed nations do not possess half of the resources God has given Nigeria, but leadership failure has robbed it of benefitting fully from the acquisition of these abundant mineral resources.

A fresh constitution should be drafted in line with what was obtained in the first republic, only this time the federating units could either be the states or the six geo-political regions. More powers should be granted the states/regions to make them very vibrant and the centre less attractive so that much attention should not be focused on the center. The states, on their part, should pay taxes to the centre in line with terms agreed upon. In this kind of arrangement, no state will now be too powerful to want to secede. Also, any individual aspiring to the office of governor of a state knows that with resource control laws to book, he is coming into office to harness the state's resources to empower his people, and not to wait for handouts from the federal government at month end.

This piece of work thus advocates that Nigerians should

exercise caution as they seek to reduce power from the center so that the same power concentration should not be recreated for the advantage of state Governors. Power should be shared proportionately to L.G.A.s, legislators and there should be independence for the judiciary to avoid abuse. The antecedents, events, body language and comments emanating from different quarters obviously indicate that Nigerians are agitating for a change from the current unproductive system.

The clarion calls for a return to the practice of true federalism is adequate and appropriate. It is an idea which time has come. A national dialogue with all sense of sincerity and purpose is necessary for Nigeria to be at peace with itself and develop.

Sources/Bibliography

Ademola, A (2009). *Ethnicity, Party Politics and democracy in Nigeria*. Peoples Democratic Party (PDP) as agent of consolidation? Department of Political Science University of Ilorin.

Fawole, A. O &. M.R. Bello, (2001). The impact of ethno-religious conflict on Nigeria's federalism. *International NGO Journal* Vol. 6 (10)211-218October,

2011.http:/www.academicjournals.org/NGOs.

Egwu, S. G. (2001). *Ethnic and religious violence in Nigeria*. Jos St. Stephen Inc. Book House.
www.christianawareness.org/factfindings.html/. 2009.

Nye J, S. (1967).*Corruption and Political Development: A case Benefit Analysis*. American   Political Science Review. 417-427.

Banfield,E. C. (1958).*The Moral Basis of a Backward Society*. Chicago: Free Press

Victor, E. D. (2008) Corruption in Nigeria: A New Paradigm for Effective Control, an article.www. Africaeconomicalanalysis.org/articles/gen/corruption dikehtm.html.

Amundsen, I. 2000. *Corruption Definition and Concepts.* This report was commissioned by the Norwegian Agency for Development Corporation (NORAD).

Encyclopedia Americana. 1999. Nigeria Corruption and Survey Study Final Report June 2003. Institute for Development Research ABU Zaria.

Chinua , A. (1960).*No Longer At Ease*. Heinemann, London Robert, L. T. (1993).Political corruption in Nigeria before independence. *The Journal of Modern African Studies.* 31(2)

Oxford Advanced Learners Dictionary.(1974). Oxford University Press ,London.

Michael, D (2001).*True Federalism and resource Control.*

http:/www.nigerdeltacongress.com/articles/truefederalis m and resourccontrol.

Nigerian Land Use Act http:/www.nigerialaw.org/landuseacthtml.

Federal Government of Nigeria. Land Management Under The Land Use Act November 2013, articleonlinenigeria.com/land.hlurb.

Federal Government of Nigeria.Land Management under the Land Use Act.
Online Nigeria.com/land

Land use act
1990.http:/www.nigerialaw.org/landuseacthtml

Land use act
1990.http:/www.nigerialaw.org/landuseacthtml

Petroleum Act.1969.
www.revenuewatch.org/sites/default/files/petroleum act.pdf.

National Waterway Decree-Nigerian Law,
1997. Source;www.nigerianlaw.org/National20
Waterways20Decree.html.

The World Fact Book.
2012,
CentralIntelligenceAgency.www.CI.Agov/library/publicati on
Nigeriaworld.com/feature/publication/peterside

The World fact book.Central Intelligence Agency.www.CI.Agov/library/publication.

Nigeriaworld.com/feature/publication/peterside.
PFN (2013).How to tackle Insecurity

 www.ngrguardiannews.com/index.php?...id...Insecurity.
Guardian , august 3rd
Kayode Are OFR 2012 Projecting Security-Lagos country
Club,Ikeja. **www.lagoscountryclub.net/.../Projecting-**
Nigeria-Security.

Nigerian Sect Boko Haram demands Islamic
state/worldnews
Http://www.theguardian.com/world/2013/may/09/Bok
o Haram-nigeria...

Nigeria,Disasters Timeline21st Century-
worldnewsAtlas.Mapreport.com/subtopics/d/countries/N
igeria/html

Pwajok, G.N.S.(2013).*Policing in a federal state: whither*
Nigeria. Distinguished lecture delivered at Jos in honor of
Dr Jonah David Jang,Governor of Plateau State@69 on
Wednesday 13th march,2013.

Asari, D. (2013).*Presidency – Its either – Jonathan or war.*
sunonline.com/news/cover/2015.May 6,2013.
Leadership Newspaper. 2013.*we-are-ready-Asari-dokubo-*
northern-youths.

Leadership.ng/news/070513/2015.may,2013.
PDP in the Post Governors Forum Election

Era,Thisdaylive.com/articles/pdp-in-the-post-governors-forum-election-era/1491266. June 2,2013.
Wheare, K, C (1959):The Federal Government, London Oxford University Press.

Birch, A. H. (1962).*Federalism Finance and Social Legislation in Canada, Austria and the United States* .Oxford University Press.
Fawole, O.A& Bello, M.R (2001).The impact of ethno-religious conflict on Nigerian Federalism. *International NGO Journal vol 6(10) pp 211-218* source;

http://www.academicjournals.org/NGOs.
Long, J. A.(1991-1992): "Federalism and Ethnic self determination, Native Indians. *Journal of commonwealth and comparative studies.*29(20).192-211.
Akande, J. O. (1998). "Protection of minorities under a federal constitution" paper delivered at the National Conference on the draft constitution Lagos Nigeria.
Rampha, S. B. (1979)." *Federalism and political instability in Nigeria*".Keynote address at the international conference of federalism Lagos. Nigeria Institute of International Affair, pp.12-25,

Goodluck Jonathan, 2012. Presidential media chat. Sunday 24th June, AIT Broadcast.

Felix, O(2012). Reconstituting Nigeria into a "True Federalism" For PEACE,Unity…article.source;www.desopadec.com/reconstituting-nigeria-into-a   true-federalism-for-peace-unity/Max, S(2205). Nigeria's First Military Coup Part 1http://www.dawodu.com/siolun5.html.

Clement, I &Ibanga, N.H. Nigeria mineral resources; A case for resource control.www.nigerdeltacongress.com/aricles/mineralresources.

Ahmed, B T (2011).*Nigeria faces bleak future without true federalism*.www.thenationonlineng.net/2011/nigeria-faces-bleak -future-without-true-   -Tinubu.

Ibrahim, B(2011).*Nigeria Need True Federalism*.Trnsparency.com/Nigeria Need True Democracy Babangida. Ibrahim, B(2011).*Begin restructuring the country now* -article. www.nairaland.com/beginrestructuring-the-country.now/babangida.
HTTP://pmnewsnigeria.com/2012/06/26/governor- jang – campaign-for-state-   police.
Oladipo, A.(2012). Speech presented by the former commissioner of police, Plateau State command during pull out /fare well parade on December 10th at Rwang Pam Stadium, Jos.
Briton, M. & Van De Walle, N.(1992). Towards Governance in Africa: Popular demands and state responses in GoranHyden, Michael Bratton (Eds): *Governance and   Politics in Africa*.pp.29.

Review of INECS STRATEGIC PLAN FOR 2007.Report of the proceedings of the Retreat held at conference hall, state library, Calabar,Cross River State.May 22nd-24th 2006. Electoral Magazine January-February 2013. TOWARDS A COMPREHENSIVE AND ALL INCLUSIVE NATIONAL VOTERS REGISTER.Fourth Edition Vol.2 No.1.

COMMENTS ON THE BOOK "2015: THE THREATS AND THE WAY OUT"

Nigeria is over fifty (50) years old as an independent nation. Before the colonial era, the territory now known as Nigeria was occupied by the empires and kingdoms brought together under the Northern and Southern protectorates which were subsequently merged to become one entity. From 1960 till date, Nigeria has experienced different political systems and arrangements: parliamentary, presidential, constitutional and military dictatorship. This book, **2015 THE THREATS AND THE WAY OUT** raises fundamental questions and extensively explores and projects into the future of Nigeria in the light of the doomsday predictions made by certain international forces that Nigeria will become extinct by 2015.

How will the Nigerian political scene look like by 2015? It is certain that the year 2015 will be a year of great expectations that will shape the destiny of the nation. The year 2015 is strategic for the reason that it is the year the nation will hold general elections. There are bound to be some alignments and realignments of some political forces and stake holders which will give birth to a new nation.

It is noteworthy that with the multi-faceted challenges facing the nation in the current dispensation, there is a very serious doubt about the ability of the nation to survive divisive and threatening wind of corruption, ethnic violence, terrorism, religious fundamentalism, economic deprivation etc.

However, the book raises a ray of hope that the nation will survive her challenges. Very few countries of the world survived a civil war like Nigeria did in the late 1960s. The hope for the future of a better Nigeria, notwithstanding, the nation should wake up to confront these challenges headlong and prove forces that see a bleak future for this great nation wrong.

This is why genuine and appropriate constitutional amendments tailored towards the installation of true federalism and emergence of visionary and incorruptible leadership for the nation should be taken into consideration. Mr. BUBA LUKA has rightly dwelled on the foregoing. I hope the issues highlighted in this book will be given a deserved attention by policy makers in navigating an excellent, progressive, and revolutionary cause the nation requires to bail itself out of the present socio-economic and ethno-religious and political mess.

TUNDE OYEBADE

LAGOS NIGERIA

ANNEXTURES

NATIONAL ANTHEM 1978 – DATE

ARISE O COMPATRIOTS

NIGERIA'S CALL OBEY

TO SERVE OUR FATHERLAND

WITH LOVE AND STRENGTH AND FAITH

THE LABOUR OF OUR HEROES PAST

SHALL NEVER BE IN VAIN

TO SERVE WITH HEART AND MIGHT

ONE NATION BOUND IN FREEDOM

PEACE AND UNITY.

O GOD OF CREATION

DIRECT OUR NOBLE CAUSE

GUIDE OUR LEADERS RIGHT

HELP OUR YOUTH THE TRUTH TO KNOW

IN LOVE AND HONESTY TO GROW

AND LIVING JUST AND TRUE

GREAT LOFTY HEIGHT ATTAIN

TO BUILD A NATION WHERE PEACE

AND JUSTICE SHALL REIGN.

THE PLEDGE

I PLEDGE TO NIGERIA MY COUNTRY

TO BE FAITHFUL LOYAL AND HONEST

TO SERVE NIGERIA WITH ALL MY STRENGTH

TO DEFEND HER UNITY

AND UPHOLD HER HONOUR AND GLORY

SO HELP ME GOOD.

However, at independence, Nigeria adopted the National Anthem which was sung from 1960 – 1978 as follows:

NIGERIA WE HAIL THEE (1960-1978)

Nigeria we hail thee,

Our own dear native land

Though tribes and tongues may differ,

In brotherhood we stand

Nigerians are proud to serve

Our sovereign mother land.

Our flag shall be a symbol

That truth and justice reign,

In peace and justice honored

And this we could as gain.

To hand on to our children

A banner without stain.

O God of all creation

Grant this our request

Help us to build a nation

Where no man is oppressed,

And so with peace and plenty

Nigeria may be blessed.

ABOUT THE BOOK

The United States of America did warn on two different occasions that if Nigeria should continue the way it is going, the country may disintegrate by 2015. A lot of other analysts have attested to that fact and current events appear to be leading to that direction.

This book analyzes the threats to the corporate existence of Nigeria and also proffers solutions. The book is both revealing and prescriptive.

ABOUT THE AUTHOR

Dashit Luka Buba is an indigene of Pankshin Local Government Area of Plateau State. He was born in Jos and grew up in the missionary town of Gindiri.

He attended Demonstration Primary School, Gindiri, from where he proceeded to Nakam Memorial Secondary School, Panyam, for secondary education. Afterwards, he went to the School of Preliminary Studies, Keffi, for I.J.M.B.E. and obtained a B.A in History from the University of Maiduguri in 2002. He is a passionate believer of the Nigerian Project.